HOW TO WRITE AN
EFFECTIVE
COLLEGE
APPLICATION
ESSAY *THE INSIDE SCOOP FOR STUDENTS*

Second Edition

HOW TO WRITE AN
EFFECTIVE
COLLEGE
APPLICATION
ESSAY

*THE INSIDE SCOOP
FOR STUDENTS*

Second Edition

KIM LIFTON &
SUSAN KNOPPOW

How to Write an Effective College Application Essay:
The Inside Scoop for Students
Second Edition

For information about this title or to order other books
and/or electronic media, contact the publisher:

Wow Writing Workshop, LLC
WowWritingWorkshop.com

ISBNs:
979-8-9859814-0-7 (print)
979-8-9859814-1-4 (eBook)

Second edition

Printed in the United States of America

Editing by Sammy Saperstein
Book design and cover art by 1106 Design
Cover/interior photography by Sam Sarkis

TABLE OF CONTENTS

Other books by Kim Lifton and Susan Knoppow

How to Write an Effective College Application Essay:
the Inside Scoop for Parents

How to Write an Effective College Application Essay:
the Inside Scoop for Counselors

FOREWORD

Shawn Felton

*Executive Director of Undergraduate Admissions
and Deputy Chief Admissions and Enrollment Officer
at Cornell University*

My first memory of meeting Wow's Kim Lifton and Susan Knoppow is on a bus. We were chatting the entire bus ride from the art museum to the hotel following the conference social on the last night of the National Association of College Admission Counseling's annual meeting in Denver. That was back in 2012; we've been friends ever since.

They were sincere, not trying to sell me a new widget or shiny object just to make a dime. And believe me, I've seen a lot of that in my years inside the admissions offices of two highly selective yet different types of schools—Cornell, now, and before that, the University of Virginia. We talked about poetry (Susan is a poet, and I love it!), swimming (Kim loves to swim), and a few of my favorite things: the Alvin Ailey American Dance Theatre and jade plants. I may have even mentioned that I used to drive the bus in college.

I was struck by how easy it was to talk to both of them. They were fun. They were real. There was no pretense. It's been a little over a decade since that momentous bus ride, and in that time I've come to realize that they really are different (and in a good way) in their desire and approach to helping students.

In fact, in all my years working at private and public selective institutions, I haven't seen anyone go as deep as Kim or Susan to gather and share accurate information from me about the college essay and its role in all admissions. They ask me good questions and listen to my answers.

It's always been clear to me that at their core, they do this work because they care about helping students like you, and in the most ethical way. They care about the written word, how it is taught, and how to reveal and protect the authentic student voice. Your voice. That's what I care most about, too.

That's why I'm here in this profession, and I appreciate people like Kim and Susan who share my mission and my values.

Let me be blunt. There's a lot of stuff out there (internet, books, webinars) about college essays. Some of it may be helpful, but so much of it is either out of context or simply inaccurate. I realize it can be hard for you to tell the difference. You've got to be careful where you go to get accurate and helpful information.

But this much I know is true: This book is the real deal because of the people who wrote it. It's easy to read, and I am certain you'll find it beneficial as you start your journey to college. Kim and Susan's spirits are in the right place, and they are exceptional at helping students like you tell your story, in your own words, and your own voice—just the way I want to hear it.

Inside these chapters, the authors define the essay, explain it within the context of the entire application process, provide useful information to help you understand what it takes to master this task, and write something appealing for me and other college admissions officers to read. They explain in detail how to understand every type of personal statement and supplemental prompt, including all seven Common Application prompts.

When you're done reading, you'll have a better understanding of why it's important to look at each essay requirement as an opportunity to share something about yourself that we might not otherwise know about you from the rest of the application package.

You can find out in this book what we—the people who admit students to our schools—are looking for in a college applicant, and how you can deliver an essay that gets noticed. But I would like to share a few of my own tips and pet peeves.

Despite what you might believe, I don't have something specific in mind when I review essays. I don't know what I want to read. But I do want you to reflect to the best of your ability in your answer to any prompt so I can get to know you a little better as I review your application.

To succeed and write an effective essay, which is the real goal, you'll have to keep your story genuine, focusing on traits and characteristics that matter to you. Only you. Not to your high school counselor. Mom or Dad. Older sibling. English teacher. Why are you telling me your story? What do you want me to know when I am done reading it? And what does that demonstrate about you?

I've been working in college admissions for a few decades. In this time, I've noticed that students spend too much time searching for stories they believe will make them sound different or unique. Please don't do that. It's a waste of your time. I don't want different. I don't want unique. I just want to know what makes you the person you are. I want to know what matters to you. I want to know what you care about. I want to know what you dream about.

If you want me or any admissions decision maker to notice you, try to worry less about standing out, and focus instead on standing up. There is a preoccupation with being different and unique among college applicants. I get it. The stakes are high, and there are so many applicants to so many schools these days. But the reality is, most college applicants are much more alike than they are different. The search for something unique to share is a long, windy road going nowhere quickly. Instead, worry less about being unique and just be you and show admissions readers who you are.

I believe that *How to Write an Effective College Application Essay: the Inside Scoop for Students* will help you do that. Most importantly, you can trust the information you are about to read.

INTRODUCTION

You've Come to the Right Place

M any students just like you come to us asking for help understanding and writing college application essays. They want to get it right, but they're not sure how.

That's because most high schoolers have had little to no hands-on experience doing this type of writing. It's generally new turf—completely different from those papers you write in English class and nothing like the lab reports you write in science class. The college essay is personal, and its purpose is to showcase who you are to someone who gets to decide if you are a good candidate for their college.

While we know that's hard to do, we hope this book will help alleviate some of the stress. The college essay does not need to be so daunting!

It shouldn't take you more than an hour or two to finish this book; it's concise and packed with information that can really help you understand the task ahead of you and give you some practical tips to approach it.

A Unique Approach to the College Application Essay

Wow Writing Workshop teaches students and educational professionals a simple, step-by-step process for writing effective college essays so students like you can stand out and tell your story.

Although many people may understand the college essay and its critical role in the admissions process, no one knows more than we do. We've been working with students and training professionals since 2009. We are a small team of professional writers and teachers who understand college admissions inside and out and follow the highest ethical standards.

We talk to admissions officers at every type of college, including large public universities, small liberal arts schools, and the Ivy League institutions. We stay in touch, listen, learn about trends, and present together at conferences. We understand the audience you are writing for.

While there's more than one way to write a college essay, there's only one type of college essay admissions officers want to read. And that's your story written in your own words and in your own voice.

This is our second book for students; it's an update of the first version, published in 2017. Our intent then, and now, is to share insight, while providing accurate information and tips, so you can be better prepared to respond to any college application essay question.

In the following chapters, we'll talk a lot about reflection. Why? At its core, the college essay is all about reflection. We'll share our approach to the college essay and clarify the mixed messages that confuse students and families.

When you are done reading this book, you will know:

- What the college essay really is, and how to write one (or 10) with minimal stress.

- How to read and break apart an essay prompt so you can understand it.

- How to respond to the prompt with an essay that admissions officers will want to read.

- What to ask reviewers to look for when they read your essay.

- How to reflect on who you are and what you want readers to know about you that might not be apparent from the rest of your application.

- How your parents can best support you. (We wrote Chapter 5 just for them.)

You should have a better understanding of how to approach college application essays by the time you complete the final Chapter 6—where we have provided some great resources.

Wow's Three Principles

At Wow, we operate on three principles that can make writing any type of college essay a whole lot easier: process, plan, and schedule. Is it fancy? Not really. But it works—every time.

Our students write essays they are proud of and that enhance their application packages, so they get the best chance of admission into their top-choice colleges. During each application cycle, we work with a limited number of students who believe in our approach. And while we don't think every person who reads this book will want to work with us privately, we know there are a few of you out there. If we sound like a fit, please get in touch through our website, WowWritingWorkshop.com.

Thank you for reading. We hope *How to Write an Effective College Application Essay—The Inside Scoop for Students* sets you on the right path.

CHAPTER 1

What Is a College Essay, Anyway?

As admission to the nation's most selective schools becomes more and more competitive, the college essay has increased in significance as well. That means to gain admission to college today, it's likely you will need to write at least one college essay—and probably more.

In a world full of information overload where anyone can post anything to any platform, you'll find a lot of buzz about the college essay: videos, blogs, books, webinars, social media posts. It's so hard to tell what's useful and what's not.

If you search the term *college application essay* (or similar terms), you'll discover plenty of material that is either irrelevant, out of context, or inaccurate. We've read and heard it all, and if you're a high school junior or senior searching for information about college essays, you've probably heard it too. If not, brace yourself.

- Some folks share templates for writing standout college essays. (Don't be fooled. This is not a fill-in-the-blank task.)

- Others promise that if you answer a bunch of specific questions, you'll be guaranteed great essays. (Questions can help you think through your ideas, but there's no magic. Writing takes time and exploration. No one can do it for you.)

- You'll find countless books filled with sample essays that supposedly got students admitted into the nation's most selective schools. (This type of claim is out of context; even the most amazing essay never got a student into college on its own.)

- Some people might tell you there are only a few types of college admission essays; if you master those, you'll be golden. (This is way too simplistic, and inaccurate.)

- Some might even suggest colleges are looking for four or five specific traits, which you should highlight in your essays. (This is not true. College admissions officers want to read an authentic story about you that is insightful, answers the prompt and showcases the trait or traits **you** want to share—whatever those traits may be.)

- The application essay is the new SAT/ACT. (We have never heard any admissions officer say this. To us, this sounds like conjecture and anxious thinking.)

When it comes to college essay advice, we understand why it can be hard to decipher good from bad, accurate from inaccurate, complete versus out of context. Just be careful. Gimmicks don't work. And you cannot shortcut this process if you want to write an effective essay that supports your case for admission.

At Wow, we teach an approach, not a cookie-cutter template. We'll always give you the facts, even when they are hard to hear or sound different from something you heard at school or read online.

We'll help you sort through the chaos.

We've been working with students for a long time, and we've learned from our experience and from our students' successes. We'll show you how to write for college admissions officers without a pre-designed structure, without reading sample essays and without added stress.

Your task: write a college application essay that gets the attention you want inside the admissions office. To do that, you'll need simple instructions, a plan from start to finish, and a schedule to help you stay on track.

Writing is a process, just like science or math.

This book will explain our writing process, called The Wow Method, but we want to be clear about what a college essay is in the first place before we talk about process.

Simply put, the term *college essay* refers to any piece of writing that a college requires as part of the admissions process. Because most schools do not conduct interviews, essays are often the only opportunity to share your unique voice.

You may hear several different terms used to describe this type of writing: personal statements, personal insight questions, supplemental essays, or short answers. We include all of them under the umbrella term, college essay.

In Chapter 2, we will explore the different types of essays and prompts. In general, no matter what prompt you're answering, your essay should be a story about you, focused on you. It's not about the children you met on a summer trip to Ecuador or your grandmother who raised you from the age of five. It should not be about your favorite novel, your Great Aunt Lucy, or the time you ran for student government. Those events and people can figure in your story, but you are the only star of your college essay.

Consider these two questions:

1. What do you want colleges to know about you that they couldn't find out from the rest of your application?

2. What do they already know?

College application readers already know from your application if you are a member of the National Honor Society, got all As but one C+ in calculus, earned a varsity letter, or served meals to the homeless on Thanksgiving Day. But they don't know if you are creative, kind, decisive, determined, or cautious.

They have no idea how your experiences have shaped you. Or how a person, book, challenge, or other experience affected you. How does your story demonstrate who you are? Did you learn something meaningful about yourself? Any type of college essay is an opportunity to show admissions what you want them to know about you.

Colleges use essays to help select a diverse class from among the hundreds or thousands of applicants whose transcripts (grades, types of classes and test scores, if appropriate) can make many students look alike. The number of essays and their length vary, depending on the colleges you apply to.

We offer a free webinar every month throughout admissions season. During each webinar, a few students will ask how long an essay should be. That depends. Essays generally range from 50 words for a short answer question to 650 for a personal statement. If you read the instructions carefully on every application, you will find the word or character count.

Some schools ask for just one personal statement. Others ask for more—or different types of writing. For the 2021-22 admissions cycle, the University of California asked students to answer four short personal insight questions; each response could be up to 350 words. The same year, the University of Texas at Austin asked for a personal statement, plus four short-answer questions. Georgia Tech required two short-answer prompts.

There are several application platforms available to families to help streamline the admissions process. New ones come and go. The most well-known is the Common Application, which in the 2022-23 cycle was being used by more than 900 schools (that number has been increasing steadily each year). We'll tell you more about the Common App essays, other types of essay prompts, and application platforms in Chapter 2.

What Do Admissions Committees
Want in a College Essay?

Since Wow opened in 2009, the answer to the question, *What do admissions officers look for in a college essay?* has not changed. The college essay has always offered an opportunity to show someone you may never meet just what kind of person you are.

When he reads personal statements, Gregory Sneed, the Vice President for Enrollment Management for Denison University, a private liberal arts college in Granville, Ohio, looks for an "intensely personal bit of character" that only an applicant can provide.

"From my perspective, unless a student interviews (which is not always an option or a requirement), the personal statement is the only place where an applicant can inject some personality into the application," Sneed says. "I've seen plenty of perfect SAT scores, and straight *As* are straight *As,* but a personal statement can truly be one-of-a-kind, in a good way."

Students (and their parents) ask us all the time if they need to sound professional in their college essays. They wonder if big words will impress admissions officers. In a word, no.

Admissions officers from every type of college and university tell us that a high school student should sound like a high school student, not a lawyer, professional writer, English teacher, or essay coach. They don't want to read something that sounds like anyone else.

Andrea Nadler, Senior Associate Dean of Admissions for Hofstra University, told us, "The college essay should allow us to use our senses to see, feel, taste and experience the kinds of things that are important to these students."

Christoph Guttentag, the Dean of Admissions for Duke University, has worked in the college world for more than three decades. We see him at college admissions conferences and look forward to chats in the hallways. Time and again, he tells us he is tired of reading essays that sound disingenuous and over-polished.

"By the time the application comes to us, many have gone through so many hands that the essays are sanitized. I wish I saw more of a thoughtful voice of a 17-year-old."

Colleges want you to be your authentic, honest, and genuine self. They are interested in you, not your mom or dad. Not your teacher or counselor. Not your sibling who is in grad school. And not the writer or editor who lives down the street.

To help schools get to know you, and to do that effectively, your college essay must be written by you and sound like you. As you might have noticed, we intentionally use the word effective when describing the type of college essay you are supposed to write.

Why? Quite literally, effective means something that is successful in producing a desired result. You are writing an essay with a purpose in mind: to help you stand out inside of the admissions office.

How Do Colleges Use the Essays?

Colleges use essays to get to know you a little bit better and to flesh out your application package. Some use them for scholarship selection, too. Assuming you are qualified academically for the school, effective essays can make a difference, tipping the balance in your favor when colleges must choose between applicants with similar qualifications.

There is no rubric for a good essay, but the ones that stand out share a few common features. Regardless of the prompt, you must:

- Answer the question.

- Showcase a positive trait or characteristic.

- Sound like you, a high school student.

- Illustrate something meaningful about you.

- Demonstrate reflection.

The key word here is reflection. The essay should teach readers something meaningful about who you are. Does the experience you write about have to be earth shattering? No. Does it have to illustrate an "aha" moment? Not at all—as long as you reflect on something that has meaning to you. There's no magic answer. No secret sauce. The essay is one (very important) piece of a holistic admission process, which generally means that as colleges decide which students to accept, they look at many different aspects of each application, from grades and test scores to letters of recommendation and essays.

"We need to dig deeper," says Calvin Wise, Director of Recruitment for Johns Hopkins University. "That's where the essay comes into play. That's where we find out more about the student. We are looking for your story. Academically, we are glad you've done well. We want to know who you are. What did your experience mean to you? How did it shape you?"

Regardless of their specific prompts, colleges want to learn something new about who you are as a person.

Tamara Siler, Deputy Director of Admission, Access and Inclusion at Rice University, believes personal statements add "needed texture."

"Quantitative factors such as transcripts and test scores only tell part of the story; a personal statement can provide context and truly show why a certain student is a better match than other clearly capable applicants."

To apply to Rice, Hopkins, and a majority of the nation's most selective schools, students must write supplemental essays specific to each school. You could be asked why you want to attend a particular college or which activity you would like to continue at college. Sometimes colleges will ask about your community or if you've experienced any academic challenges.

You might also be asked to answer a creative prompt. The list goes on and on.

We'll delve more into common types of supplemental prompts in Chapter 2. For now, we want to emphasize that every time you are asked to answer a question in writing as part of your application to college, you need to take it seriously. Colleges would not ask you to write these essays if they didn't want to hear what you have to say.

Admissions officers we've talked to over the years are delighted when a story rounds out an applicant's package. They appreciate an essay that helps them understand who the person is. They want to put a face to the application file.

What turns them off? Stories that are not genuine, do not answer the prompt, or fail to give them any insight into the applicant's character. One thing we hear consistently from admissions officers from coast to coast: They don't like it when students try too hard to impress them, or when students write essays that seem forced, heavily edited, or inauthentic.

Remember, take this task seriously. Don't whip off your essay(s) the night before the deadline. Treat every essay as the opportunity it is meant to be. In other words, don't wing it!

A college essay can make a difference in helping colleges say yes to your application. At a moderately selective school (60% admit rate and higher), where more applicants hear yes than no, students who meet certain academic requirements will generally be admitted. For students who don't quite meet the standards but are not far off, the essay can push a student into the admit pool.

At a selective school (40% admit rate and lower), where more applicants hear no than yes, essays are even more critical. They help distinguish one student from another. The essays are even more significant at a super-selective college, where admit rates dip below 15 percent.

We'll talk more about the world of college admissions in Chapter 4. No matter what happens next, the essay is not going away and it will continue to be significant inside an increasingly holistic admissions process. There are a lot of moving parts in this process, and nothing is guaranteed. You might never know how many applicants have the same GPA and test score as you in any given year, or how you measure up in other ways.

Any type of college application essay is an opportunity to make yourself more three-dimensional in the eyes of admissions officers. How do you do that? Use the essay space to highlight one or more character traits you want to share with colleges.

You can begin by answering these questions:

- What do you want colleges to know about you apart from the rest of your application package? (Think traits and characteristics, not experiences or activities.)

- What story can you share that illustrates the trait you want to share, and also answers the prompt?

Volunteer trips to other countries can be great experiences for many students, but a story about the trip might not make an effective college essay. In the same vein, getting free breakfasts at school because your family cannot make ends meet might tug at readers' heartstrings but might not necessarily make a strong college essay, either. At the same time, either story could work if the essay demonstrates something meaningful about you.

You can write about anything you want, as long as it highlights a personal trait, answers the question, and shows insight.

Here is an example of a story that tugs at the heartstrings and did work.

We worked with a student who lived on ramen noodles and rice every day for a year. She loved to dance and had to take three buses every day to get to the studio, where she also worked to pay the activity fee. She wrote a compelling story about riding the bus for hours every day to work toward her dreams. It was effective because the story demonstrated hard work and determination.

Here is an example of another effective story—about learning to mow the lawn—that demonstrated hard work and determination without tugging at any heartstrings. It was just as beautiful. This student had assumed it would be no big deal when her dad suggested teaching her how to do it. But it was really hard. She stuck with it for several weeks until she mastered the task.

We've read countless stories from students who experienced something meaningful when dealing with a parent or friend who died or was sick. But we've read just as many stories from students who experienced something meaningful from everyday experiences, like learning to dive, teaching a scared child to put their face in the water, or having a disagreement with a parent.

While we don't believe you need to go so deep that you land far outside of your comfort zone, it is critical that you reflect enough to let colleges see who you are and how you think.

The Best Essays Are Simple and Personal

Admissions officers say the best essays are simple and personal. They don't read applications hoping to hear a certain type of story or to discover if a student possesses one of those "top traits colleges want to see in your college essay" that you might read about on the internet.

They don't care what trait you demonstrate or how your story is structured. Rather, they like all types of stories, as long as they are genuine, show reflection, and answer the prompt. In fact, colleges are often less critical of student essays than you or your worried parents might assume.

We realize it can be hard to write about yourself, especially when the stakes seem so high. But we also know you are more than prepared for this task. If handled properly, college essays can make your application come to life above the piles and piles of applicants. As a bonus, writing these essays can also leave you feeling empowered, confident in your abilities, and certain of your words.

You might be wondering, *Do colleges really read every application essay?*

Yes, college admissions teams read your essays. Sometimes one person reads them, but often, a few admissions readers will review your work—or even an entire committee.

Truth be told, colleges would not ask students to write application essays if they did not use them to help make important decisions about your future.

Unlike your accomplishments, which will be evident from the rest of the application (in the spaces provided for activities, jobs, grades, and scores), the essay is a place to broaden a college's understanding of who you are. It's extra credit, a chance to share something they don't know about you that can make your application pop.

In so many ways, the college essay is much more of a thinking task than a writing task. If you can think about what the prompt is asking and what you want to share about yourself, you can write an effective essay. Sure, colleges want to make sure your writing is strong enough to succeed in college, but that's not the main point of this task.

No one else besides you knows how you think or what goes on inside of your head. That's why we start the college essay process by asking our students questions about what's important to them, what traits they want to showcase, and what they want readers to learn about them. Our students draft their essays after they are clear about their reasons for writing each story.

This can be challenging because it has nothing to do with how well you perform in English class. In general, high schoolers come to the admissions process with little or no experience with this type of writing. While English teachers know how to recognize excellent writing, they look for something different from admissions counselors. Most (not all) do not know how to teach—or have not been trained to teach—personal statement writing for the college admissions audience.

We don't offer essay review services anymore, but when we did, we worked with many students who had asked us to read the drafts they wrote in English class. They wanted to make sure the essays were ready to click Send. Sadly, while most of the essays earned As, there were just a few that were ready to be submitted to colleges. With few exceptions, we sent them back to the drawing board. The essays were beautifully written, but they usually missed the point and lacked real reflection.

And that's what colleges want: reflection. Admissions readers are not grading essays for powerful prose and sentence structure. They just want to know who you are.

Like it or not, the personal statement is part of the college application experience. The essay can help, and sometimes it can hurt. According to Stefanie Niles, the President of Cottey College, "I have definitely seen a poor essay, submitted with an otherwise solid application, keep a student from being admitted. I have also seen a particularly strong essay, submitted with an application containing some red flags, tip the scale toward a positive admission decision."

If you want your application to stand out, make sure you write an essay that reviewers will take seriously. It won't be as hard as you might imagine, but it does require time, strategy, and effort.

The writing process will be easier when you understand the task, can be introspective, and know what you want colleges to know about you beyond the material shared in the rest of the application. As we move through the next few chapters, keep reflection and voice in mind. Both are crucial when writing a personal statement.

Our Mantra: It's Your Story. Your Voice. Your Words.

We've already mentioned that beyond the obvious transcripts, relevant test scores, and academic rigor, admissions officers need ways to get to know applicants on a more personal level, and that most do not have the time or resources to conduct personal interviews. The essay can substitute for that face-to-face meeting. But without an interview, how will you convince someone you don't know that you are the right choice for their school?

First, think about your audience. It is not your parent, your counselor, or your high school English teacher. Your audience is a college admissions officer whose job includes reading piles of essays every day.

So, how can yours possibly stand out? Listen to your writing voice. Your unique voice will allow your essay to connect with readers. What do we mean by that? When we use the term "voice," we are referring to the writing's natural tone, sound and feel. The most successful essays sound like the people who wrote them.

Your story, told in your own voice and in your own words, will show readers something genuine about you, something they can't get from test scores and grades and long lists of activities.

What does your voice sound like? How will you recognize it? That is one of the first issues we address with the Wow Method, the step-by-step writing process we use with every student.

Just like your speaking voice, your writing voice is distinctive. Are you witty? Be witty. Are you serious? Be serious. Do you write in short, concise sentences? Then write that way in your essay. Do you like to use long, complex sentences full of vivid details? That style should show up in your essays, too. Don't get distracted by the thesaurus; it won't help you find words you use every day. Don't try to sound like Ernest Hemingway or Toni Morrison. And don't try to sound like your parent, older sister, or science teacher. Just be yourself.

Consider the story of Scott, a smart young man from the Midwest. He was visually impaired and wanted to show colleges how resourceful he was. He did this through a story that demonstrated how he learned to self-advocate for accommodations in school.

Scott's first draft was very good. He answered the prompt, and the first draft sounded like him. Scott just needed to flesh out some content and add a few details. We took him through a couple writing exercises to do that, and he continued moving in a positive direction.

But something happened between drafts. When we reviewed his second draft, Scott's voice had disappeared. We noticed a few awkward transitions that did not match the writing style we

15

saw in his previous work or in the rest of the draft. The revised essay now included a formal introduction and a conclusion.

It became clear that someone had helped Scott craft his second draft. He got too much help!

We asked Scott if someone had worked with him, and after hemming and hawing and insisting the essay was much improved, he fessed up. He was not confident with his own writing, so he asked his father to fix it. We asked Scott to circle the parts of the essay that his father had written (even though we knew!). Scott's father had written the introduction, plus a few bad transitions and the conclusion. To be blunt, his dad ruined his essay.

We asked Scott to write his own draft without his father's help. He did, and Scott's voice returned. His story was genuine. The essay was beautiful. His voice—and his alone—set him apart.

He was qualified for his top-choice school; the essay strengthened his case during an exceptionally competitive year. Scott was thrilled he got in. We never heard from his dad, but Scott's mom thanked us for boosting her son's confidence in his writing. She loved his real story.

Your Voice Will Set You Apart

Take a moment to think about your voice. Your voice can set you apart, too.

When you tell your story, in words you use every day, your essay will capture your voice. That doesn't mean you can't sound sophisticated. It does not mean you cannot use big words, either. But only use big words in your college essay if you use them in your everyday life. Some people think it helps to use humor in your essay. Sure—if you are funny—and if you want to show that side of yourself. But don't force it.

Remind yourself that colleges want to read an essay about you, written by you, that sounds like you.

A word of advice about accepting help from your parents and other well-meaning adults: There is a fine line between getting assistance and allowing someone to write a sentence, paragraph, or entire essay on your behalf. Parents, like Scott's father, may not always be able to tell when they've gone too far, but admissions officers know when a piece of writing does not sound like a high school student, and they don't like it.

That's why adults should never revise, write or otherwise "fix" your essay. If they do, the essay will sound like an adult who is trying to write in a teen's voice. Instead of improving your case for admission, they will be hurting you because the admissions team will know you did not write it all yourself.

Like most of the admissions folks we know, John Ambrose, the Director of Undergraduate Admissions at Michigan State University, has strong opinions on this topic. He says the college essay is the one item that can separate you from everyone else in the application pool.

"I look for genuineness of character, unique flair of personality, identifiable traits of a leader or follower, team player, and someone who has the capacity to add to the rich diversity of our campus and our traditions," Ambrose says. "Be your most authentic self. Students put a lot of effort into trying to convince admissions officers who they think we want to see. But authenticity is always appreciated."

Everyone has a natural writing voice. No two are the same, but they all capture the spirit of their author. Over the years, we have had some favorite lines that really reflect the true voice of the student who wrote it.

Read a few of our favorite lines from Wow students, and you'll get the idea:

- I got my first pair of skates before I could walk.

- I jumped into an empty Dumpster and scrubbed it with a heavy-duty brush using Pine Sol and Comet cleanser.

- My body trembled as I heard the words, "If you hear the siren, you have 15 seconds to save your life."

- When I was in tenth grade, I waged a campaign to save my district's middle school French program.

- Because I am short, I managed to wiggle my way through the crowd to the front to see the list.

- I wanted to be a normal kid, just like them, not the kid with a sick dad.

- It was an overwhelming smell that reminded me of a thrift shop filled with unwashed clothing.

- I love the sound of the boat straining under the pressure of eight perfectly synchronized oars, and the copper taste in my mouth when I pull my absolute hardest.

These examples tell us something about the writer. They are written in different styles and different voices. Your voice cannot be copied; it's your signature.

Once you are confident with your voice, you will be able to focus on what you want colleges to know about you: the traits and characteristics that define you. When you are done with your final draft, your essay should illustrate those characteristics.

Mundane Moments Matter

We love essays about ordinary moments. Colleges do, too.

Consider our student, Ari, who decided to ditch gymnastics for the swim and dive team at his high school. He had never been a diver, but he wanted to give it a try. He anchored his essay around something ordinary: learning to do a simple dive. He messed it up terribly—23 times, in fact. But on the 24th time, and an hour after team practice ended, he did it. It was not a perfect dive. He described it as mediocre at best. But Ari felt accomplished because he finished what he started, even though it was challenging. Ari demonstrated determination, grit, and perseverance through this story that mattered to him. Best of all, he loved his essay.

Trust us, a college essay does not need to be written about something big. You do not have to rescue an infant from a house fire, get a million downloads for an app you developed, or teach a child who is scared of the water how to swim to impress admissions officers.

Frequently, we learn enduring life lessons during ordinary moments—the moments when our best and most authentic selves emerge. That's why some of the most effective college essays we read focus on the most mundane moments:

- An aspiring baseball player watching his cousin take endless batting practice

- A boy and his sister stuck in traffic

- A talented dancer choosing to drop all but a few of her dance classes

- A high school junior trying out for the pom-pom team at her new school

- Two brothers on a bike ride through their neighborhood

- A young person cooking dinner for younger siblings

Does that mean a strong college essay must be written about a mundane moment? Not at all. If you know what you want readers to learn from reading the essay, your story is just an illustration of that characteristic or quality. The topic can be big or small, as long as you show reflection, sound like yourself, and answer the question the college asks.

Students ask us all the time how to tell the difference between a good college essay and a bad one. We tell them the term "good" is relative. What looks good to an English teacher will not necessarily satisfy a college admissions officer. The admissions officer is not looking for a polished essay, written, revised, and edited for *The New Yorker*. We prefer the word effective over good.

In its simplest form, an effective personal statement will have a **theme** that answers these two questions:

1. What happened? (your specific story/topic)

2. Why does it matter? (the trait/traits your story shows)

Let's say the summer you worked as a lifeguard, you surprised yourself with your ability to teach children to swim.

"My summer working as a lifeguard" is too broad a topic for your essay. Instead, zero in on that idea with a specific moment or experience like, "The afternoon I finally got Ally to swim across the pool without crying." We call this the anchor story. You can add lots of context later, but the anchor story gives you somewhere to start. It should illustrate something meaningful about you—the traits that are your answer to "Why does it matter?"

Many other types of application essays can be judged by theme as well. While the anchor story will naturally take center stage, readers will also understand why the writer chose to share it and what they're trying to show about themselves.

Admissions officers are not going to get excited over a piece of writing that beautifully details an experience, then adds a generic sentence at the end, stating that the writer learned something significant. Nor will they enjoy a five-paragraph essay with an introduction, thesis statement, supporting paragraphs, and a conclusion. For college admission, your story needs no introduction or conclusion. There is no particular structure or type of story to imitate for the college essay; the best essays emerge from the writing and thinking process.

A few years ago, one of our students illustrated his determination with a simple story about memorizing the parts of the gastrointestinal tract to ace his anatomy final. Another girl wrote about finding her passion for nature in a community garden where she was pulling weeds. A boy with an autism spectrum disorder blew us away with a powerful story about his problem-solving skills. He forgot his cello for an orchestra concert and improvised his performance with a bass guitar. This story impressed admissions officers at his top-choice school, and his admission letter even praised the essay.

While these stories were beautiful, none was perfect. The college essay is not about perfection. Not even the most selective colleges expect brilliant prose from a teenage applicant. They know they are dealing with kids, so they often will cut applicants like you some slack. At the same time, they want to see some effort and a healthy respect for the rules of written English.

The essay is the ultimate place to show colleges who you are. We encourage you to reflect and honor your voice so you can confidently share your stories.

As you begin the process, always keep in mind:

What are you writing? A story about you

Who are you writing for? College admissions counselors

Why are you writing it?

- to illustrate something meaningful about yourself

- to demonstrate how you think

- to help admissions officers round out your application package

- to show that this college is a good fit

Your essay should be:

Specific: Don't write about your entire summer working on a construction site. Choose an important moment or other small piece of your experience, then demonstrate why that moment matters.

Genuine: Speak in your own voice. Don't try to be funnier, smarter, or more creative than you already are. Make sure you sound like yourself.

Direct: Say what you mean in plain language and try to make your writing clear and easy to follow.

Personal: Even if your experience seems mundane, the fact that it happened to you makes it unique.

Exercise: *Finding Your Voice*

We developed our own warm-up writing exercise that has become a Wow signature. Before our students start writing anything, we ask them to complete this free write called *Finding Your Voice*. It's an introduction to our process that teaches students how to write a personal statement for college admission. (You can read more about our process in Chapter 3.)

The exercise has two parts. To complete it, you'll need a piece of paper, pen or pencil, or a computer. You can even do this on your phone.

This exercise is meant to be a quick, inviting warm-up to the writing process. More importantly, it will help you identify and think about your writing voice. Before you start writing your essay, it's important to take a moment to recognize what your writing voice sounds like naturally when the stakes are not so high. Keep in mind, this is the authentic voice admissions readers want to see; it will help them get to know you.

Let's get started.

Part One

Prompt: What did you do this morning from the moment you woke up until you left your home?

Write fast, and do not judge what you write. Don't even read it as you go along. Just keep moving forward.

- Open a new document or use a notebook and pen.
- Set a timer for 10 minutes.
- Write about your morning.
- When the timer stops, stop writing and read the instructions for Part Two.

After you open a new document or a clean sheet of paper, quickly write down as much as you can recall using all your senses. Be specific, but don't worry about making sense or sounding clever. You can write fragments, sentences, lists, or run-ons. It doesn't matter because you are not writing an essay; you are just capturing details.

Part Two

Your writing voice is unique and often shines through when you relax and write freely. Look back at what you wrote about your morning and find three segments that truly sound like you. Each one can be anything from a short phrase to a multi-sentence description. They don't have to be exciting or clever; they just have to sound like **you**. For example:

- Something you always say, do, or think.
- A description of something that screams "my house!" or "my room!" or "my mom!"
- A phrase you like, a detailed description, or something clear and specific that sounds just like you.

When you find your segments, highlight, bold or underline them. These are examples of your writing voice. This is what you sound like when you are not trying too hard to be clever or creative. This is the voice you should write in when you begin to compose your application essay. Keep it in mind as you work on the essay.

CHAPTER 2

Getting Started:
Understanding the Prompts

Kirsten, a high school junior at the top of her class, was hoping to land a coveted spot at the most selective university in her state. She contacted Wow for coaching on the three required essays for that school, plus assistance with a few optional short-answer prompts.

At first, she seemed confused because she didn't have any ideas for essay topics. She wanted to know if she was doing something wrong.

During our initial meeting with Kirsten and her parents, her mom suggested a few ideas. Kirsten could write about the science fair or why she wants to be a doctor.

We listened. We wanted to be respectful. Then we gently interrupted and suggested slowing down.

We explained that students need to do their own work, which includes picking a topic of their choosing. Parents should never suggest ideas.

To begin the process, Kirsten needed to understand what the college was asking her to do with her application essays.

We helped her understand the prompts (or essay questions) and told her she could pick a topic later, after she knew what traits and characteristics she wanted to share with the school.

Her relief was palpable. Kirsten's shoulders dropped, her jaw relaxed, and she smiled.

What should I write about? is one of the most common questions we get from students who are about to start writing their college essays.

Students and parents want to know if admissions officers have favorite topics (no), or ones they are sick of (they get tired of stories that don't share anything about the student, but they don't get tired of stories that share something meaningful and answer the prompt).

Before we get to topics, it's important that you grasp exactly what the admissions team is trying to find out about you in an essay. In this chapter, we are going to teach you how to read and understand prompts.

To start, let's talk about how to break apart a prompt.

Ask yourself these two questions:

1. What is the college asking me?

2. Why is the college asking me this question?

Admissions officers tell us the single biggest mistake students make **is not answering the prompt.** You don't want to make that mistake.

So, take some time to read each essay question closely and make sure you understand it before you start writing.

You're not alone if you thought an essay's topic was the first thing to consider. That's what students talk about on websites where just about anyone can share an opinion without much expert moderation. It's not your fault if you did not know this! But let's be clear, it's hard to answer a question if you don't understand what it is asking. We'll put it in context first.

Look at these instructions for the personal statement on the Common Application:

The essay demonstrates your ability to write clearly and concisely on a selected topic and helps you distinguish yourself in your own voice. What do you want the readers of your application to know about you apart from courses, grades, and test scores? Choose the option that best helps you answer that question and write an essay of no more than 650 words, using the prompt to inspire and structure your response. Remember: 650 words is your limit, not your goal. Use the full range if you need it, but don't feel obligated to do so. (The application won't accept a response shorter than 250 words.)

These instructions are followed by seven prompts to choose from. It does not matter which one you choose; the key question is always: What do you want colleges to know about you? This is your opportunity to make your voice heard, to teach readers something new about who you are beyond grades, test scores, and activities.

Here are the seven prompts the Common App offered in the application year 2022-23:

1. Some students have a background, identity, interest, or talent that is so meaningful they believe their application would be incomplete without it. If this sounds like you, then please share your story.

2. The lessons we take from obstacles we encounter can be fundamental to later success. Recount a time when

you faced a challenge, setback, or failure. How did it affect you, and what did you learn from the experience?

3. Reflect on a time when you questioned or challenged a belief or idea. What prompted your thinking? What was the outcome?

4. Reflect on something that someone has done for you that has made you happy or thankful in a surprising way. How has this gratitude affected or motivated you?

5. Discuss an accomplishment, event, or realization that sparked a period of personal growth and a new understanding of yourself or others.

6. Describe a topic, idea, or concept you find so engaging that it makes you lose all track of time. Why does it captivate you? What or who do you turn to when you want to learn more?

7. Share an essay on any topic of your choice. It can be one you've already written, one that responds to a different prompt, or one of your own design.

Let's take a closer look at Common App Prompt 1: *Some students have a background, identity, interest, or talent that is so meaningful they believe their application would be incomplete without it. If this sounds like you, then please share your story.*

Ultimately, an essay responding to this prompt is not about a student's background, identity, interest, or talent; it's about why that background, identity, interest, or talent matters to the student.

Admissions officers read these essays to find out something they don't already know about you. They can tell from the application if you are on the lacrosse team or in the school orchestra, or if you worked as a researcher, a hospital aide, or a bagger in a grocery store. What they don't know is why those experiences are meaningful to you or what you learned about yourself. They have no idea how you have changed or what traits you rely on, either.

The essay is the place to share such insights. And your story will grow out of the process of writing it.

You can respond to this prompt by sharing any type of story—a description of a significant conversation, a time when you realized something personally important—anything that truly and vividly demonstrates who you are. You do not need to climb a mountain, deliver meals to front-line healthcare workers during a pandemic or travel to another country to write a compelling story. Babysitting, playing virtual D&D games with friends, making meatballs with Grandma, or navigating an icy highway works, too.

The why (the characteristics your story highlights) is more important than the what (your experience).

No matter the prompt, before choosing a topic, ask yourself this question: *What do I want colleges to know about me beyond grades, test scores and extracurricular activities?*

We explain in detail what each Common App prompt means in Chapter 6. Along with the Common App, other popular applications require their own personal statements. While all of them ask students to reflect on specific aspects of their lives, each uses different prompts and word limits. As you read through the different prompts below, you will likely notice plenty of similarities and differences between them.

Another application, the Coalition for Access, Affordability and Success, is integrated within Scoir, a platform with many college advising tools that is free to all students and free to Title I-eligible schools. The application includes a personal statement with several prompt choices, asking students to choose one and write about 500 to 650 words.

Here are their prompts for 2022-23:

1. Tell a story from your life, describing an experience that either demonstrates your character or helped to shape it.

2. What interests or excites you? How does it shape who you are now or who you might become in the future?

3. Describe a time when you had a positive impact on others. What were the challenges? What were the rewards?

4. Has there been a time when an idea or belief of yours was questioned? How did you respond? What did you learn?

5. What success have you achieved, or obstacle have you faced? What advice would you give a sibling or friend going through a similar experience?

6. Submit an essay on a topic of your choice.

During the 2022-23 application season, the University of California asked students to choose four out of these eight Personal Insight Questions (up to 350 words for each):

1. Describe an example of your leadership experience in which you have positively influenced others, helped resolve disputes or contributed to group efforts over time.

2. Every person has a creative side, and it can be expressed in many ways: problem solving, original and innovative thinking, and artistically, to name a few. Describe how you express your creative side.

3. What would you say is your greatest talent or skill? How have you developed and demonstrated that talent over time?

4. Describe how you have taken advantage of a significant educational opportunity or worked to overcome an educational barrier you have faced.

5. Describe the most significant challenge you have faced and the steps you have taken to overcome this challenge. How has this challenge affected your academic achievement?

6. Think about an academic subject that inspires you. Describe how you have furthered this interest inside and/or outside of the classroom.

7. What have you done to make your school or your community a better place?

8. Beyond what has already been shared in your application, what do you believe makes you stand out as a strong candidate for admissions to the University of California?

Many institutions in Texas use the ApplyTexas application, with its own personal statement questions. Here are the 2021-22 ApplyTexas prompts (each school application specifies which prompt to answer; essays should be between 500 and 700 words):

1. Tell us your story. What unique opportunities or challenges have you experienced throughout your high school career that have shaped who you are today?

2. Some students have an identity, an interest, or a talent that defines them in an essential way. If you are one of these students, then tell us about yourself.

3. You've got a ticket in your hand—Where will you go? What will you do? What will happen when you get there?

Many other state universities also ask their own personal statement questions on their independent applications. While we cannot predict what the admissions process will look like in the future, all evidence indicates the essay will remain an important piece of the college application puzzle.

The Supplements

In addition to personal statements, you likely will need to write supplemental essays specific to the individual schools you apply to. Here are some tips for approaching a variety of supplement types. You can also apply the same techniques we described for personal statements when parsing supplemental prompts.

"Why College X?" or "Why This School?" Essays

Often students misunderstand the Why College X? prompts—and miss out on an important opportunity to improve their case for admission. We don't want that to happen to you, so please read this section carefully to find out how to nail this challenging essay.

Questions about why you want to attend a particular college often look like these from current and past years' applications:

Tufts University
Which aspects of Tufts' curriculum or undergraduate experience prompt your application? In short, "Why Tufts?" (*100-150 words*)

New York University
We would like to know more about your interest in NYU. What motivated you to apply to NYU? Why have you applied or expressed interest in a particular campus, school, college, program, and or area of study? If you have applied to more than one, please also tell us why you are interested in these additional areas of study or campuses. We want to understand—Why NYU? (*400 words maximum*)

Cornell University College of Engineering
For you, what makes Cornell Engineering special? Why do you
want to attend Cornell Engineering? (200 words maximum)
    In every case, your answer to a Why College X? prompt
needs to address three important areas:

1. The school: What attracts me to this college or program?

2. The student: What do I want readers to know about me?

3. The stories: How does what I know about the program
    mesh with what I want readers to know about me? How
    can I illustrate this intersection? (stories/anecdotes)

Many students have very little idea what a school offers
academically, socially, or culturally. Sometimes students choose
a college because of the location or its status. This is not what
admissions officers want to know. They may need to know you
will be comfortable in a big city, but they are more interested
in their school and what the college or program offers. Do
you have the chops to succeed academically? Are there any
clubs and activities to support your interests? Why do these
factors matter to you? Depending on how familiar you are
with the school, answering these questions may require some
research (online, in-person visits, talking to current students
or alumni, etc.).
    Each year, we meet many young people who insist that a
school is perfect because they feel at home inside the football
stadium and love listening to stories around the Thanksgiving
dinner table from Dad, Aunt Lisa, and Cousin Diana, all enthu-
siastic and accomplished alumni. Colleges want students to be

comfortable for many reasons, but this type of answer is never sufficient. It does not answer the prompt.

Community Essays

Some schools want to find out how students might contribute to the campus community by learning about how they participate in their current community.

The University of Michigan has asked this type of question for several years. It is a typical community essay prompt:

Everyone belongs to many different communities and/or groups defined by (among other things) shared geography, religion, ethnicity, income, cuisine, interest, race, ideology, or intellectual heritage. Choose one of the communities to which you belong and describe that community and your place within it. (300 words maximum)

Our friend Kim Bryant, U-M's Assistant Director of Admissions, Visitor Experience & Engagement, spends a lot of time reading and reviewing essays—thousands of application packages each season. She has spent decades inside the admissions office in Ann Arbor and loves hearing student stories.

She knows what she wants from a community essay: "We have an amazing, vibrant, thriving community made up of students in athletics, strong academics, research, over 1,200 student clubs and organizations. We want to know what applicants do in their community, church, high school, synagogue, and mosque. What are they going to do on our campus to make a difference in the world?"

Here are a couple more prompts that ask students to write about how they have contributed, or hope to contribute, to a specific community.

University of Pennsylvania

At Penn, learning and growth happen outside of the classrooms, too. How will you explore the community at Penn? Consider how this community will help shape your perspective and identity, and how your identity and perspective will help shape this community. *(150-200 words)*

MIT

At MIT, we bring people together to better the lives of others. MIT students work to improve their communities in different ways, from tackling the world's biggest challenges to being a good friend. Describe one way in which you have contributed to your community, whether in your family, the classroom, your neighborhood, etc. *(200-250 words)*

Diversity and Inclusion Essays

Some colleges present opportunities for students to discuss how they will contribute to a diverse and inclusive campus. While these prompts can sometimes sound similar to the community essays described above, pay attention to what each school specifically asks students to focus on in their essays.

Duke University

Duke University seeks a talented, engaged student body that embodies the wide range of human experience; we believe that the diversity of our students makes our community stronger. If you'd like to share a perspective you bring or experiences you've had to help us understand you better, perhaps related to a community you belong to or your family or cultural background, we encourage you to do so here. Real people are reading your application, and we want to do our best to understand and appreciate the real people applying to Duke. *(250 words maximum)*

Pomona College

We believe that everyone has something to contribute and receive from a diverse community. Why is belonging to a diverse and inclusive college community important to you? *(200 words maximum)*

Rice University

Rice is lauded for creating a collaborative atmosphere that enhances the quality of life for all members of our campus community. The Residential College System and undergraduate life is heavily influenced by the unique life experiences and cultural tradition each student brings. What life perspectives would you contribute to the Rice community? *(500 words maximum)*

Activity Essays

Often, colleges like to know more about how a student spends their time than the sentence or two that students include on the activities section of an application or resume. When asked, "Which activity would you continue in college?" or "Tell us about one significant activity," students need to expand upon the activity by explaining what they like about it, what they find engaging about the activity, and why this is important to them.

As with all essay opportunities, make sure you know why you are sharing a story. If you write about tennis because you won six championships, that information is likely already in your application. If you write about how hard you worked to get along with your new doubles partner, and as a result you became a better team player, that's something readers wouldn't already know.

One of our students wrote an amazing activity essay about learning the value of hard work when he cleaned out a dumpster; it was not the easiest task to get while working at a summer camp. But he was asked to do it as part of his job in the kitchen of the overnight camp he had attended for many years. His colorful description of the activity, along with what he learned, showed how hard he worked under the worst of circumstances. His essay revealed his character. That's why it worked. And that's why we loved it.

Every activity essay, no matter how short, offers a space to share something new and meaningful about yourself and your interests. Consider these examples:

Georgetown University
Briefly discuss the significance to you of the school or summer activity in which you have been most involved. *(Approximately one-half page, single-spaced)*

Vanderbilt University
Please briefly elaborate on one of your extracurricular activities or work experiences. *(200-400 words)*

Harvard University
Please briefly elaborate on one of your extracurricular activities or work experiences. *(50-150 words)*

Princeton University
Briefly elaborate on an activity, organization, work experience, or hobby that has been particularly meaningful to you. *(Please respond in about 150 words.)*

Influential Person Essays

The prompts on college applications are not always as straight-forward as they appear. Consider the "influential person" essay prompt, which might look like this: Indicate a person who has had a significant influence on you and describe that influence.

Colleges do not want to just read stories about Aunt Rose, a beloved first-grade teacher, or the student's great-grandfather who invented the crinkle potato chip. Instead, you need to write about how this special person helped shape you, what you gained from the relationship, and why it matters to you now.

It is admirable if Aunt Rose saved five children from a burning house or won the Presidential Medal of Freedom. But what does that have to do with you? Were you one of the kids she saved? Are you a volunteer firefighter because of this experience? If not, let Aunt Rose apply to college on her own. She might even earn a scholarship for her heroic acts.

Issue Essays

Even if a college asks students to discuss an issue (racism, poverty, domestic violence, world hunger, gun control) that is relevant to them, admissions officers still want you to reflect on that issue from a personal perspective. Consider the "issue essay" prompt, which might look like this: Discuss some issue of personal, local, national, or international concern and its importance to you.

Are you passionate about the environment? Do you follow politics like a veteran pundit? Are you a vegetarian or an advocate for the elderly? These are admirable issues, but unless you can explain what you have done because of this great concern, this essay won't shine; it won't be effective. Why did you become a vegetarian? How has it affected your daily life? What insight have you gained while teaching Mom and Dad to cook tofu? Answers to questions like these demonstrate reflection.

University of Virginia
Rita Dove, UVA English professor and former U.S. Poet Laureate, once said in an interview that "there are times in life when, instead of complaining, you do something about your complaints." Describe a time when, instead of complaining, you took action for the greater good. *(Roughly 250 words)*

Creative Essays

Students generally either love or hate creative essays. Here are three sample prompts from the University of Chicago, the leader of the creative, provocative prompt:

1. What if the moon were made of cheese? Or Neptune made of soap? Pick a celestial object, reimagine its material composition, and explore the implications. Feel free to explore the realms of physics, philosophy, fantasy . . . the sky is the limit!

2. What's so easy about pie?

3. It's said that history repeats itself. But what about other disciplines? Choose another field (chemistry, philosophy, etc.) and explain how it repeats itself.

In addition to a personal statement, UChicago asks students to write several supplemental essays, including one creative essay, about 1-2 pages long.

Students who attend UChicago like questions like this. But if you can't bear the question, it might be a sign that UChicago is probably not a good fit.

The idea is to have some fun with this essay. "Write it any way you want," the school tells students. "We think of [the creative prompt] as an opportunity for students to tell us about themselves, their tastes, and their ambitions. They can be approached with utter seriousness, complete fancy, or something in between."

Other schools offer creative prompts as well. These samples come from current and past application seasons.

University of Vermont
Which Ben & Jerry's ice cream flavor (real or imagined!) best describes you? *(500 words maximum)*

Stanford University
What historical moment or event do you wish you could have witnessed? *(50 words maximum)*

Covid Prompts

The Common App, Coalition App, and some colleges, like the University of Texas, added prompts during the Covid-19 pandemic, some optional and some required. The Common App's prompt is optional. Colleges ask these types of questions to find out how you lived through challenging circumstances like Covid or other natural disasters in a genuine way.

Common App Covid Prompt
Community disruptions such as COVID-19 and natural disasters can have deep and long-lasting impacts. If you need it,

this space is yours to describe those impacts. Colleges care about the effects on your health and well-being, safety, family circumstances, future plans, and education, including access to reliable technology and quiet study spaces. (*250 words, optional*)

This prompt, or one like it, may remain on the Common App and other applications; it might not seem relevant for you. If you have something to add to your application surrounding a natural disaster of any kind, this is a good place to share that information. But remember, no whining and no gloating. This is a place to share information you want colleges to know about you.

The Common App added this question to the Additional Information section, where students have always had the opportunity to share other information about circumstances like an extended absence from school, long-term illness, or a significant decline in grades. If you feel you have something to share in the Additional Information, or another optional section, it is recommended you discuss your circumstances with your high school counselor or another trusted admissions expert.

There's no need to manufacture challenges or heroic efforts in an answer to any prompt.

The Covid prompt and all supplemental essays offer chances to share something new with colleges and give a more complete picture of who you are. Make the most of this opportunity.

CHAPTER 3

Writing Your Essay
With Confidence

Before we start working with our students, we tell them: "This is your journey, so own the process. When you are done, you will be a more confident, empowered writer, ready for college and your future. Trust yourself!"

We want to share this message with you, too. It does not matter where your story takes place, how large or small it is, or what you did. You matter. Why you did something matters. What you learned matters. How it changed or affected you matters.

Answer the prompt with a story illustrating the trait you want to share in a way that shows how you think about your character and helps admissions teams get to know you a little better. You should trust your own words, style, and voice.

Every year, we work with students who tell us they cannot write; they don't believe in themselves. We know better. We challenge them to follow our approach. It works. Every time.

Why? With simple instructions, anyone can learn how to write.

Do you think you can't write? Nonsense.

David was one of those students who lacked the confidence to write his essay. Applying to college was stressful; writing the essays paralyzed him. He came to Wow convinced he just couldn't write.

David had good grades in math and English, did well in his AP classes, and got high scores on the ACT. He spoke clearly and articulately. The boy who said he could not write was a sports reporter for his high school newspaper.

Like so many students feeling pressure to get into college, David's fear of writing this essay prevented him from getting the job done.

"Can you think?" we asked him.

"Um, yes," he said.

"Well, then, you can write."

If you can think, you can write, too.

We talked with David about what mattered to him, and why. Why did he want to go to college? What did he want admissions to know about him? What were his defining traits and characteristics that he wanted to share with colleges? In other words, what made him tick?

David said everyone already knew he was a talented hockey player and that he worked hard to be so good. But he had another side few could see. He was kind and compassionate with a soft spot for children with disabilities. He wanted to write about that because colleges had no other way of knowing this side of him.

We brainstormed ideas based on those characteristics. One of his ideas involved a "hockey story." But David was afraid to write about hockey because "everyone" told him to avoid writing about sports.

We told him the advice about sports stories was not correct—or, more likely, out of context. He should not write about sports

46

or any experience; he should write about himself, showcase his preferred traits, and reflect on his topic. Any topic. Even hockey. If he answered the prompt with a story that was focused, showed insight, and was meaningful to him, the essay would work.

After the explanation, David relaxed and started talking about his cousin Danny, who had Down Syndrome. Danny would come watch David play hockey. That made him so happy.

In the end, David anchored his story around the moment Danny held up a homemade sign to cheer him on during a game. It got to David. It motivated him. He teared up on the ice. "I just wanted to score one for my cousin," David said.

David's story highlighted David's compassion and kindness, something that colleges would never have known. He used it for two different college applications. It was his idea, and no one else could possibly duplicate it. He was admitted to his two top choices.

The night after he completed his personal statement, David's mom called. She had never seen her son this excited about anything other than girls or sports. He finally believed he could write.

David trusted himself, wrote confidently in his own voice, and he liked what he heard.

You can do the same.

Choosing a Meaningful Topic

Many students get excited over college essay ideas they think will get them some attention inside the admissions office, without giving much consideration to what the college essay prompt is really asking.

Starting with a topic in mind may seem like a good idea, but really, it's not. If you want your college essay topic to grab the reader, and you've been racking your brain, trying to decide which idea is best, take a few steps back and put the idea aside.

As we explained in Chapter 2, it is critical you understand the prompt before you start kicking around topics or worrying about what you think colleges want to hear or topics you think will be so unique. You also want to make sure you know what you want to share with colleges before thinking about story ideas.

Your job—your only job—in your college essay is to share something meaningful about yourself that answers the prompt.

That's it. It's not as hard as you think.

Be Prepared

Preparing yourself to write college essays is one of the best gifts you can give yourself during a potentially confusing and stressful time. The sooner you begin, the better. Contrary to popular belief, writing is not the biggest challenge here. Exploring who you are, what matters to you, and how you exhibit those traits or characteristics in the world is the important part.

We'd like to take some of the pressure off. When we help our students focus up front, the rest of the process moves along much more smoothly. Figuring out what makes students tick at the beginning of the process is essential—and the first step toward reflection. For you, that means before you start writing, choosing a prompt, or picking a topic, you should take some time to decide what you want colleges to know about you.

We've been hosting a college essay class each month between February and November for years. Hundreds of students sign up each month. It's free, and we ask students to submit their most pressing college essay questions.

We answer as many as possible during the 60-minute webinars.

The No. 1 question is always a variation on topics.

- How do I find a great topic?

- Which topics are off-limits?

- Which topics do colleges really like?

- Which topics stand out?

- Can I write about _____?

Too many students get hung up on the topic of the college essay, long before they are ready to start the writing process. They look for activities that might lead to stories and devote a lot of time talking about their experiences and accomplishments. This is why college essays can seem so difficult. Students start in the middle of the process without even knowing they skipped the first part.

What Makes a Great Topic?

Have you been thinking about what makes a great topic? Do you think you know what you will write about? If so, slow down. We suggest that you take two steps backward if you plan to start your college essay process with a topic in mind. Instead, focus on a few traits and qualities that make you great. How would you describe yourself?

- Are you kind? Funny?

- Are you resourceful?

- Are you compassionate? Curious? Patient?

- What are your best qualities?

We've already told you that college applicants don't always stand out because of grades, test scores (if applicable) and unusual experiences. But it is so important that we are going to repeat it. We want you to remember it. Your college essay matters. A lot.

To make it memorable, you need to put in some effort and think about yourself in a deeper way than you may have before. We understand identifying your own best features can be hard. Students are often more comfortable talking about accomplishments or the future. This all makes perfect sense. How much time have you spent wondering how you made it to this point in your life? Perhaps during the Covid pandemic, when we were all quarantined, you started missing life as you knew it. Or maybe you realized some things were more important than others.

Even so, it's unlikely you spent much time—if any at all—writing about yourself in a reflective way. No worries. The college essay is the place to do that.

Let's Try to Reflect a Little

Ready to reflect? Begin by answering these questions:

- What three words would your best friend use to describe you to a new student who came to your school?

- What do you like to do when you are not at school?

- What do your friends say about you? Are you a problem solver? Do you like a challenge? Are you resilient? Committed to a cause? Focused?

- How would you fill in this blank: *I'm the kind of person who* _____.

- If you were standing on a stage, and five people you never met were in the audience interviewing you for your dream job, what would you want them to know about you that they wouldn't know from reading your resume?

- What makes you great?

You can answer these questions alone or discuss them with your parents, siblings, or friends. In our experience working with students, we find that getting started is the biggest challenge. Let's face it, writing about yourself is hard. We get it. You cannot do a Google search to gather content. And you cannot learn about yourself from a textbook.

So, what should you write about? You might have some ideas already, or you might not. It doesn't matter.

Trust the process to guide you.

The key question here is not "What do colleges want to hear?" Instead, reframe the question and ask yourself, "What do I want readers to know about me?"

If you want to show your dedication and work ethic, you could possibly write about the time you made an elaborate diorama for a friend's birthday, or you could discuss studying all night for a geometry final.

Whether you write about shopping for sneakers with your little brother or building houses for residents of a mountain town, the topic is secondary to what it illustrates about you. Select a topic that will allow you to share something genuine about yourself.

Consider prompt #2 from the Common Application: *The lessons we take from obstacles we encounter can be fundamental to later success. Recount a time when you faced a challenge, setback, or failure. How did it affect you, and what did you learn from the experience?*

This prompt asks you to choose one incident or time when you faced an obstacle. The incident itself is not what matters, though it will be the springboard for the second half of the question. Your readers are most interested in how this experience affected you. They want you to reflect and share what you have learned.

Interview or Journal . . . or Not!

You can come up with ideas many different ways. Some people like to let their minds wander or make notes. Others ask themselves questions or ask a friend to interview them. Some record themselves talking out loud, and others just mull it over for a while. Once you know what you want readers to learn about you, think about stories or experiences that might illustrate those characteristics.

You might also try keeping an informal journal.

If you choose this technique, think of your journal entries as though they were quick snapshots from your phone—something you might post on social media or in a text. Their purpose is to jog your memory and remind you of an experience, not to capture it in spectacular detail.

If you try to record everything that happens on your trip to the Grand Canyon or every thought about your summer job as a swim teacher, you'll give up after a day or two. On the other hand, if you jot down, "Sunset with Brian and Sarah. The sky looked like it was painted in watercolor," you will remember that evening forever.

If you scribble, "Ally finally put her head in the water! I threw the red plastic ring to the bottom of the pool, and she went straight down for it," you'll also remember the way the sun hit the diving board and the lady in the lounge chair who sat by the pool all summer with iced tea and a trashy novel.

As professional writers, this is the type of journaling we do, too. Sure, we sometimes write pages and pages, but we also collect scraps of experiences and moments.

Be Specific

Whether completing these exercises takes an hour or a week, it's time to get specific.

In Chapter 1, we discussed how "My summer working as a lifeguard" is too broad a topic for an essay. But if you wanted to write about your ability to teach children to swim, you could focus on something like, "The afternoon I finally got Ally to swim across the pool without crying." This scene is your anchor story, the specific experience that illustrates something meaningful about you.

As you brainstorm ideas for your essay, keep in mind what you want readers to know about you. If the event is only meaningful because it happened in an exotic location, then the story is about the location and not about you. If the experience would have been equally meaningful if it took place in your grandmother's backyard, then it's a story about you and could make a terrific college essay. Before you choose a "best idea," you need to consider several possibilities. You might be surprised by which story you choose to tell.

Stay focused on a moment. Think of yourself as a storyteller, with you as the narrator of your own story.

How Spencer Nailed His College Essay

Spencer had a lot of ideas for topics when he was working with us on his personal statement. Spencer did not know how to write about himself; he was an extremely shy and introverted boy. He attended a faith-based day school. Religion—a huge piece of his school experience—baffled him.

Spencer talked about his confusion about his beliefs quite a bit at home, which worried his mom. In fact, she called us to make sure we would tell him he could not write about his beliefs. We told her we would take him through a process of discovery and see where it went.

We explained the essay is never really about a topic, which illustrates something meaningful about the student. This anchor story gives the student a place to start, allowing exploration and reflection on what's important—the student who writes it.

Spencer wanted colleges to know that he used to be shy, but now he felt like a leader. He was determined and compassionate.

He had a list of ideas to support the traits he wanted to share with colleges. Because he was adamant that he also wanted to write about God, we did what we always do, and began the conversation where he wanted to start it: Bible class. If he could answer the prompt, share something meaningful about himself and show reflection, the topic would work.

Spencer wrote about the time he raised his hand in Bible class and blurted, "I am not sure I believe in God." This was something he was told to believe in. Over the years, he went with the flow. But he was ready to figure out what his beliefs were for himself.

When he spoke up, Spencer felt relief. He was brave and honest. And then, slowly, a handful of other students raised their hands and talked about their own beliefs and their own confusion. The teacher praised him. The conversation that followed was deep. Even better, this was the first time Spencer felt like a leader. He initiated a difficult yet significant conversation.

"I always felt uncomfortable talking about God," he wrote in his essay. "It was scary telling the teacher and my peers that I didn't know if I believed in God."

Spencer wrote a gorgeous story anchored around that pivotal moment when he raised his hand and communicated his feelings. It answered the prompt and exhibited leadership through a few of his best traits: determination, integrity, and courage.

What Are Your Best Traits?

So, are you still thinking about your best traits? Do you know which ones you want to share with colleges? It's okay if you don't know just yet.

Let's try to find out.

Answer the question we introduced in Chapter 2: "What do I want colleges to know about me beyond test scores, grades and extracurricular activities?"

Think about your traits and characteristics, not activities, honors, or awards.

Your answer will guide your essay.

We cannot emphasize enough that in highly competitive college admissions, where many students can look the same on paper, decision makers depend on personal narratives to broaden their understanding of who you are, not just what you have accomplished. So, before you start writing your college essay, spend some time thinking about your best traits and characteristics. Then, find stories to illustrate those traits.

Your parents can help you reflect on your life experiences, so you can dig a little deeper. Your friends can tell you what they like about you. Feel free to reach out to your siblings, too.

But you are in charge of the topic. And only you! Others might suggest ideas, but unless it comes from within and is sincere, it won't work.

The people who know and love you can tell you what they like about you and what they see from raising you, living with you, or hanging out with you. They can remind you that you are industrious and thoughtful. But they should never tell you which trait to feature in your essay, or which story is the best example to highlight it. If someone tries to influence your story, you might consider listening and respectfully ignoring their advice.

Colleges want to know who you are and what you want to share with them. It's all up to you. No one else. When you can think about your life experiences and reflect on what they mean to you, you will be able to write your college essays with confidence.

As writing teachers who are also respected experts on the college essay, we know the boundaries of guiding students. We know how much to help and when to back off. We know intuitively when it is time for our students to be done.

Your parents and others with good intentions might feel pressure to do more, rather than less. The pressure comes from outside forces that you and your parents may not even recognize.

Our process helps students reflect so they can write stories that resonate with them. We put our students in the driver's seat. We guide the process, which is easy to follow, and we keep them on schedule.

When you are ready to begin your essay, remind yourself that the subject of the essay (you!) is more important than the topic (the experience you choose to write about). Your reflection on that topic will give meaning to the essay and help you get the attention you deserve inside the admissions office.

Our Secret: Process. Plan. Schedule.

When we work with students or train high school counselors and other professionals who help students apply to college, we talk a lot about process. Because the secret to getting a college essay done effectively, quickly, and with ease is to have a plan to get it done and a schedule to follow.

At Wow, we operate on three principles: Process, plan, and schedule.

- Process: Our process is our magic. Our approach is simple, with clear instructions to help you succeed.

- Plan: We help students plan ahead so they can calmly write essays that will enhance their application.

- Schedule: Each student works one-on-one with a professional writing coach, following a proven schedule that we can adjust to meet individual needs. Most of our students apply to four or more schools, which means they have to write approximately 10-15 essays. We make it easy to get it all done.

Whether or not you work with a Wow coach, we want to help minimize the confusion surrounding the college essay, make this task less draining, and provide useful information to get started. You should always have a plan and schedule before you start writing, no matter how many essays you need to write.

Throughout this chapter, we describe the main principles we use to guide our students. If you are working on your own, you can use these principles to guide your own essay process. The following sections will help you think about how to approach your own college essay journey.

Content First, Then Structure and Polish

This graphic on the following pages illustrates the Wow Method, the process we've developed and honed over more than a decade of working with students and training counselors. We break up the process into three phases: Content, structure, and polish.

The Wow Method
Your College Essay In Ten Simple Steps

CONTENT

01: Understand the Prompt

Before choosing a topic, make sure you understand what the prompt is asking and how the essay fits into the application. Focus on what readers already know about you, as well as what they can't find out from the rest of your application.

02: Brainstorm Ideas

Consider several topics. For each, consider the prompt, the story idea, and the positive characteristic(s) the story illustrates. You might be surprised by which one you choose.

03: Focus on Theme

Every essay needs a theme to help you focus. The theme includes both 1) What happened? (What story are you sharing?) and 2) Why does it matter? (What will readers learn about you?)

04: Free Write for Details

This is your chance to capture details, focusing on the What happened? aspect of your theme.

05: Write Draft 1

Draft 1 is a content draft. It's okay to go over the word limit. Don't over-think it or try to make the essay perfect. You'll focus on structure and polish later.

06: Review Prompt & Theme

We read first drafts with the prompt and theme in mind, then give writing exercises to help students focus the essay and add details where needed. This review is for content only.

CONTENT + STRUCTURE

07: Write Draft 2

Step back to review the work you've completed so far, from Step 1 through Step 6. Then write draft 2, focusing on both content and structure.

08: Review Content and Structure

For second drafts, we add notes in the margin, pointing out what works and places for improvement, based on each student's willingness and ability to take the essay further.

CONTENT + STRUCTURE + POLISH

09: Write Draft 3

Step back again and read the essay with fresh eyes. Tie up loose ends and make sure it is clean, but don't revise your work beyond recognition.

10: Final Review and Proofread

We read final drafts for clarity and consistency, focusing on grammar, spelling, and punctuation. Perfection is not the goal. College applicants should sound like high school students, not professional writers.

Content: Steps 1-6

As you begin the process, the goal is to get everything down on paper. You don't need the perfect opening line, and you shouldn't worry about keeping everything in the right order just yet. In fact, you won't even start writing your first draft until Step 5.

Why?

Preparation is paramount. As we have detailed in this chapter, it is critical that you understand exactly what you are trying to achieve before turning your ideas into an actual essay. By the time you finish that first draft, the content of the essay should be absolutely clear. Step 6 offers an opportunity to confirm that the content is all there.

Structure: Steps 7 and 8

Next, we concentrate on structure: making sure every part of the essay is exactly where it belongs. You should check and recheck that your essay works from every possible angle. Even as you begin to focus on structure, content is still important here. Through revision, you will likely find new and better ways to express yourself.

Polish: Steps 9 and 10

After working on structure, it is finally time to polish. This is where you make sure your writing is clear and sounds exactly how you want it.

Content and structure are still in play, but now you will move from revision to editing and proofreading.

One of the most important takeaways from this chapter is to take the writing process one step at a time. Don't start with preconceived notions about what makes a good essay. Trust the process.

Content comes first, which includes breaking down the prompt and brainstorming ideas you want to share with schools. As you move through the revision process, focusing on structure, then polish, your essay will grow stronger and stronger.

Make a Plan

Wow's ten steps help students put their stories on paper in their own words and in their own voice. We never tell anyone what to write. Instead, we teach our students how to draft compelling personal essays. And we help them create plans to start writing and get done smoothly.

Because we plan ahead, we consider activities, vacations, the number of schools selected, and the number of essays required. Our students don't spend entire weekends writing essays for multiple schools.

Before we start working together, we ask students a lot of questions, and we plan together. Then we break down the tasks required to write each essay into manageable steps, so students can get the work done efficiently and effectively. We provide a detailed plan for completing any student's essays in plenty of time. While the number of essays varies by school, Wow students write an average of 10–15 essays for 4–5 schools.

Our coaches work with students on one school at a time, providing support for every essay for that school, from brainstorming ideas through multiple drafts and final review.

If you are completing your essays independently, we also recommend working on one school at a time so that you can make steady progress without overwhelming yourself. We hope you finish the journey to college with beautiful stories and a great sense of pride.

Schedule

We use a four-week schedule with every student for the first personal statement, generally the Common App essay or a personal statement for the Coalition App, ApplyTexas, or the University of California system.

The first week is administrative, giving the student and coach time to prepare for the real work ahead. Weeks two and three focus on content creation and revision. Week four features polish and catch-up. We assign the most time-consuming tasks for the weekend. We keep students moving quickly through the essay, so they don't lose momentum.

While we appreciate that not all students are the same, we have yet to meet a student who cannot follow simple instructions, stay on track with a detailed schedule, and meet deadlines when they know them up front. Exceptions happen. But they are rare. And when that happens, we adjust our schedule.

On average, students spend 10-15 hours writing the first personal statement. The first supplemental essay can be challenging, but after that, students typically move along at a faster pace. As you consider how and when you will work on your essays, consider your upcoming school, social, and family responsibilities, as well as any application deadlines. You don't want to set yourself up with unrealistic expectations, but at the same time, no matter what's going on, your life probably gets busy sometimes. Working hard to stick to your schedule will pay off in the end. Compared to dragging out your essays, consistently making progress will ensure a much more manageable, and perhaps enjoyable, process for you (and your parents!).

Ready to Write?

If you're curious about how well our process actually works, consider Michael, a young man who worked with us on his college essays. At first, like so many students we meet, he truly believed he could not write. He changed his mind after finishing his personal statement. He wrote this to us after he was accepted to college. "I didn't know I could write. My friends just help each other, and they end up emailing [their essays] back and forth to three or four friends for review. They just keep rewriting without any real input. You taught me a process so I can do this again by myself. You helped me come up with my own ideas."

Here's a comment from a parent in New York whose daughter got into all eight schools she applied to: "I'm convinced her essays made a big difference, and we are so grateful for everything you did for her."

Finally, we got some kudos from Peter, a transfer student who was already a skillful writer when he came to us: "Wow did much more than help me craft strong and effective essays for my college applications, though they certainly did that too. They taught me to approach writing in a new way and gave me a process that I will keep with me forever. It is hard to explain just how useful their approach has been, but within minutes of sitting down (and I was skeptical at first), I was in awe of its efficacy."

As we've shown you, we spend a lot of time in Wow's opening steps making sure our students know why they are writing the essay and what they want to say. We make sure that first and foremost, our students understand the prompt and can illustrate something meaningful about themselves in their response. If you put adequate time into preparation, your writing will flow more naturally. Best of all, the essays will turn out better. That's what happens to students who take the time to get it right at the beginning. Once you decide what you want to share with colleges and have chosen an essay topic, you will be ready to start writing.

To begin, find a quiet space to write. It's best to be alone when you write your draft because writing your college essay is not meant to be a group activity. You might be tempted to ask an adult you trust for help. We understand. But when you write alone, your voice will come shining through. Our students sometimes ask us which words to use, what types of sentences colleges like, and if there is a way to make their writing sound smarter. The most common question we get comes in the very beginning of the process: Where do I start? We'll tell you what we tell them: Use the words you already know. Colleges like the words and sentences you choose. Start your story anywhere. The beginning. The middle. The end. It doesn't matter. Just start.

As you write that first draft, keep in mind that the essay can be revised later. For the first draft of an essay, you need to get content down on paper. Structure will emerge through the revision process. There's no need to get everything in the ideal order. Don't worry about the opening line. Not in the first draft. At this point, we encourage our students to write too much, then cut and change words and sentences later.

Once the first draft is done, you can ask someone you trust to review the essay for content only. Ask your reviewer to read it without a red pen in hand or their hands on the computer keyboard. Before they read, tell them what the essay is about and why you chose this topic. You also need to provide your reader with the right questions, so their comments are useful.

We ask these questions when we review our student essays:

- Is anything missing?

- Is the essay's purpose clear?

- Does it have a solid theme that answers the questions: *What happened?* and *Why does it matter?*

The first draft is not supposed to be ready to submit. While you don't need to worry about perfection, it's critical you make sure you've answered the prompt. You and your reader should both double-check the prompt. If the prompt asks you to reflect on an experience and its influence on you, be sure you have talked about both the experience and its effect.

We don't mark up first drafts. Rather, we respond with comments and questions and additional writing exercises to help focus the content or add more details, context, or reflection (depending on the specific essay). At this point in the process, we don't correct grammar and spelling because we don't know if those exact words will end up in the final product.

After the first draft review, you can continue to develop your essay through freewriting and revision. As you revise, try to let go of any preconceived notions about what makes a good essay. It's important to just write. Don't fall in love with your first opening line or the entire first draft. Be open-minded. Be willing to be surprised.

Many students find that their essays go in wonderful and unexpected directions as they revise. When you understand that revision involves "re-seeing" an essay, it feels less like fixing something that is broken and more like a process of discovery.

Students sometimes try to shortcut the revision process, but their essays inevitably stall, rather than evolve and improve. When students take the time to do it right and think like a writer, they are pleased with the results. After one of our students, Sarah, got to college, she sent us a note saying that learning how to revise made her a better writer. She told us, "I learned to transform something I have written into something totally new. Writing is no longer taking apart something that I made but creating something bigger and better than I had before."

You can have an equally meaningful experience with writing and revision. Once the first draft is complete, our coaches can generally get a student through to the final draft in two to four additional revisions, but that number is not set in stone. While there is no right or wrong number of drafts, at some point, you will need to let yourself be done. Just remember, colleges are not looking for expertly crafted documents; they want to learn more about what makes you tick. Your job is to present the admissions committee with a personal statement that showcases your positive character traits and shares something about you that they wouldn't have known otherwise.

You'll know you have made it to the final draft once the content is in place, the structure has emerged, the essay clearly responds to the prompt, and the writing flows from beginning to end. That's your cue that it's time to polish. You can now ask someone to check to see if you've crossed every *t* and dotted every *i*.

If you'd like a family member, friend, or teacher to review drafts of your essay, please share the checklist below with them.

Content Review:

- Does the essay answer the prompt?

- Can you tell why I chose this topic?

- Is the essay about me, or is it really about the place, person, or experience featured in the essay?

- Does it illustrate a trait I want to share with colleges?

- Does it tell colleges something meaningful about me that is not clear from the rest of my application package?

- Does the essay sound like me?

Structure Review:

- Does the first paragraph make you want to keep reading?

- Does the essay move smoothly from beginning to end?

Polish Review:

- Does the essay use the same verb tense throughout?

- Have I avoided sentence fragments and run-on sentences?

- Is the punctuation correct and consistent?

- Is every word spelled correctly?

You've made it this far. Give yourself a pat on the back.

While our private services may not be for every student, a few of you might want to go beyond this book and work with our coaches. If that sounds like you, please visit our website, WowWritingWorkshop.com, and see what we have to offer. If not, enjoy the book. It's packed with useful information to help you get started the right way.

CHAPTER 4

Competition and Confusion
Inside the College Admissions World

The competition to get into the nation's top colleges gets tougher every year, but that's not because students are smarter or more qualified than they were 5, 10, or even 20 years ago.

It's a simple matter of impossible math.

Year after year, more students apply for the same number of available spaces at the most selective schools in the U.S. It is impossible for everyone to get in—no matter what's going on in the world.

So, how can you get into that dream school when the odds are stacked against most applicants? Good question. We provided some tips for gaining an advantage through your college essays in Chapter 3. In this chapter, we'll explain the essay's role within a holistic admissions process. Holistic generally means that as colleges decide which students to accept, they look at many different aspects of each application, not just grades and test scores.

This process emphasizes academic achievement through rigor of coursework, grade trends, test scores (including AP and IB exams), application essays, class rank, letters of recommendation, activities inside and outside of school, special talents, and individual circumstances, like disabilities, illness, and family or financial situation.

Because college essays are just one aspect of the application, we want to help you understand how admissions works overall, and also address some of the major changes to admissions that began during the Covid pandemic.

With more perspective on how admissions officers function, you will be better prepared to write effective essays that answer any type of prompt.

Still, please put the essay into its proper context. Whether they are more important now than they were a decade ago is not the point. If you are asked to write a personal statement, a short answer, or a supplement of any kind, take it seriously. Put your best effort into every single essay you write.

How the Covid Pandemic Changes
Everything We Thought We Knew

At press time, we were just getting back to some sense of normalcy at Wow following 18+ months of massive changes in admissions and everywhere else. So, let's take a moment to discuss the Covid pandemic. Because it's too big to ignore. As you know, between 2020 and 2021, we were all quarantined to some degree; school, social activities, volunteer work, and even college recruiting went online. We created pods of people we deemed safe to see.

In a blink, everything changed for us, for colleges, high schools, for you, your friends, everyone we know, and everyone you know.

Without much notice, high schools and college campuses closed to in-person learning. College administrators acted swiftly, moving in-person recruiting and outreach activities to virtual platforms. We saw new interactive online communities take center stage as the numbers of podcasts, webinars, and social media events exploded.

Admissions crews were basically grounded (many to their ad hoc home offices), and colleges had no choice but to plan more robust outreach and recruitment efforts to connect with students using virtual tools.

What happened next was surreal. Administering ACT/SAT exams became nearly impossible, which led to a mass exodus from mandatory testing requirements. By the spring of 2021, there were 1,680 schools that decided not to require ACT/SAT scores for fall 2022 applicants. Some were test optional/flexible and others, test blind. Essentially, test optional/flexible means students get to decide whether to submit an ACT or SAT score with their applications. Test blind means a school does not accept any test scores and will not consider them as part of the review process.

Before Covid, standardized testing companies were already under the microscope due to claims that the tests are racially biased, and some colleges have announced their intentions to remove the testing requirements permanently. It could take years to sort it all out.

The question remains: In this environment, will the essay become even more important? Some admissions insiders say yes. Others say we'll see. Will colleges ask for more writing? Perhaps. Can we gaze into a crystal ball and predict the future? Nope. No one can.

But here's what we do know: Increased access to admissions through virtual tools amid a new landscape of test-optional admissions contributed to record numbers of applicants in 2021 at a variety of schools. These included the most highly selective schools (like the Ivies), private schools (like New York

University, Williams, Coby), and popular public institutions (such as the University of Virginia, the University of California system, and the University of Michigan).

Highly selective private institutions across the country that accept the Common Application saw a 22% average increase in applications for the incoming class of 2025. The admit rates also decreased substantially, making it more competitive than ever for students applying to these super-selective colleges. Specifically, MIT was at the top end of the upward trend, with a 66% increase in applications; MIT admitted just 4% of applicants (more than three percentage points down from the 7.25% the previous year). UCLA's apps rose by 28%; UCLA was at 12.4%—down from 14.4% the previous year. In 2020, Cornell offered admission to 10.7% of its applicants. A year later, that number decreased by two percentage points to 8.7%.

The same year, for the first time, admissions rates dropped below 4% at several institutions. Harvard offered admission to 3.4% of its applicant pool. Princeton was right behind, admitting 3.9% of applicants.

"This was a year like no other," according to Shawn Felton, Cornell's Executive Director of Undergraduate Admissions (who penned the foreword to this book). "The lives of our applicants— and their experiences as high-school students—have changed. As a result, the way we reviewed applications also changed. It was especially important to be flexible this year; understanding and empathy have been key considerations for us."

The Essay's Role in This Changing Admissions Landscape

One mom looking for advice on the application process told us she was certain her daughter would need to write stellar admissions essays if she were to apply to college without test scores. The girl had great grades, and she took challenging classes, but she was not a good test taker. She had no interest in submitting test scores.

We explained that while the essay has always been important, it would not replace anything else. Without test scores, admissions teams will use everything else they know about a student to decide if they have what it takes to succeed at their universities.

Yes, the essay is important, perhaps critical. But academic rigor (grades, difficulty of courses) is, and always has been, the most important aspect of the application—more important than test scores. An amazing essay can support your case for admission if you are qualified for the school you are applying to. But it will not rescue a lousy transcript—or help you or any student who is not qualified to get an offer of admission.

What you are seeing now is exactly what we've been telling students and parents for more than a decade. The essay is vital and an opportunity to make yourself seen and heard inside the admissions office, and you should treat it that way.

Put effort into every essay you write for every college on your list. With or without test scores, you should always write the best essays you are capable of.

Look Inward, Focus on What You Can Do

We want you to succeed, and we want you to have the right tools to do so. We've been working with families and professionals for more than a decade. No one knows more than we do about the college essay. We share our knowledge with students, parents, and professionals all the time.

While change is a constant inside admissions, the race to get in is challenging every year for every group of applicants. It's been this way for decades, long before Covid shut down life as we once knew it. And, fair or not, we don't have any reason to believe it's going to get easier any time soon to gain admission to a name-brand school with impossible odds.

Sigh. Breathe. Do yoga. Go for a swim or a walk or meditate. Do whatever you need to do to remain calm. It's time to look inward and focus on what you can do, and not what you cannot do.

It's understandable to want to try to find some new, special strategy to get an edge. But you'll never discover a magic solution. No one ever does. And you'll just get more and more frustrated and stressed-out if you continue to go down this path.

We don't want you to feel that way. We'd like to make things easier, perhaps a little calmer. Because you deserve that.

First, it's important to recognize why admission to so many schools, maybe even your big state university, is so competitive.

Because it is so hard to get into the top name-brand schools (think Stanford, Harvard, Columbia, Cornell, UCLA, MIT, Vanderbilt, Northwestern, University of Chicago, to name a few), students who are qualified for the most selective colleges look elsewhere to improve their chances. They use modern technology to apply to more and more schools than applicants in previous years.

Today, students can apply to multiple schools, whether they choose 5 or 15, using one of several streamlined applications that make the process almost seamless (though no less expensive). The most popular is the Common Application, which was used by nearly 900 colleges and universities in 2021 and grows every year. The Common App makes applying to college so easy that students frequently check boxes for schools they might normally ignore if more effort were required.

This practice helps colleges increase their applicant pool. It works well for schools because it makes them look more selective. If a school can accept only 1,200 students and 6,000 apply, the admit rate—or the percentage of students the school accepts—will be 20%. If 12,000 apply, the college will enroll the same number of first-year students, but the admit rate will plummet to 10%. On paper, it will look like this college has become more selective ("We accept only 10% of applicants."). This practice can be challenging for students like you who just want to get into a good college.

Texas has its own application, called ApplyTexas, as does the University of California system, New York's SUNY schools, and several other state networks. The Coalition for Access, Affordability and Success went live in spring 2016. Fewer schools use it, and most of the schools that accept it also use the Common Application or their own applications.

These days, it may be hard to get in, but it's almost too easy to apply to multiple schools.

To see how the ease of applying affects the admit numbers at popular colleges and universities, look at the University of Michigan, which began accepting the Common App in 2010. That year, applications jumped by 25%; U-M received a record 39,584 applications, and its admit rate dropped to 38.9%—the lowest percentage since 2005. Five years after joining the Common App (2015), applications to U-M surpassed 50,000, and the admit rate plunged to 26.3%. By 2020, applications had jumped to more than 65,000, bringing the admit rate down to 22.9%.

There are about 4,300 two- and four-year degree-granting colleges in the U.S., according to the National Center for

Education Statistics. As of 2019, there were nearly 20 million students enrolled in college in the U.S. As you can see, there are a lot of schools beyond the name-brands, and if you want to go to college, there is more than one that could be right for you.

You Are More Than a Number

You might notice that the name-brand schools dominate the news, social media, college ranking lists, and conversations among you and your friends. While these schools tend to get the most applicants, there are always plenty of spots for students at the thousands of colleges out there. If you conduct your own research, attend college fairs, and talk to your school counselor, you'll be able to develop a list of choices that are appropriate for you.

The increasing competition to get in is not all bad news for students. Colleges, under pressure to be more inclusive and accessible, are beefing up recruiting and marketing efforts in under-represented communities. If you keep your ears open, you'll probably hear about unfamiliar schools as your journey to college continues. And don't forget that while students need colleges, colleges also need students. When you create a list, we recommend applying to some colleges that say yes more than no.

Did you know that some of the lesser-known schools give away the most cash in scholarships? Yes, you can get noticed. Just be realistic, and once all the hard work is done (such as getting an A on the calculus final), you will want to focus on your essays.

With more and more students applying to the same schools, you'll need to help admissions officers see beyond the numbers on your application and transcript. That's why essays are so important.

As we've mentioned, it's unclear exactly how college admissions will continue to change in the coming years. No matter what happens next, one thing remains constant: Writing matters.

Every year, the National Association for College Admission Counseling surveys admissions officers throughout the nation. For the past two decades, the factors that admissions officers have used to evaluate applications have stayed largely consistent. Students' academic achievements—which have included grades, strength of curriculum, and test scores (if applicable)—constituted the most important factors in the admissions decision. Application essays have also moved up on the list, right beneath grades and test scores.

At most schools, everything comes into play: grades, essays, activities, letters of recommendation, and possibly test scores. For you, the applicant, this can be confusing because you may not know what colleges actually expect in each of these different areas.

There's always been something going on that makes applicants and parents nervous. But it's out of your control. So, no matter where you plan to apply, try to focus on what you can control, like grades, activities, and writing your essays. One thing should not be confusing: The essay is important, and in some cases, critical, inside the admissions process.

We cannot emphasize strongly enough that colleges are interested in character as well as grades. That does not mean you should seek out specific character traits you think colleges want you to have. If you share your most meaningful traits and characteristics in college essays, you will naturally stand out.

In your college essays, highlight the positive traits that make you who **you** are—not the person you wish you were, or the person you may believe has a better shot at getting in. Trust yourself. Trust the things you value.

Do you have Ivy League ambitions? Hoping for a spot at your favorite Big Ten school? Or are you eyeing a great college right in your backyard? A meaningful college essay, written in your words and your voice, can help you promote yourself and make your case for admission.

We have interviewed a lot of admissions officers from major universities and small colleges alike, and they all say the same thing. Without exception, they advise students and parents to relax and focus on the things you can control. That's easier said than done. We know it.

If you are applying to a school that accepts the ACT or SAT, you take it several times, and that score doesn't rise accordingly, you may not be able to do anything about it. But you can improve your grades and take classes that are both challenging and appropriate. You can also write a stellar story about yourself in your application essay.

Several years ago, a friend took his son, a talented member of his school's rowing team, on a tour of elite East Coast colleges and universities. We asked him to let us know what he heard at those schools regarding admissions essays.

Most college representatives mentioned the essay during their presentations, but MIT took the message a step further. While talking about the quest for the perfect ACT or SAT score, the admissions representative reminded parents and prospective students that test scores merely indicate whether a student is academically ready for freshman courses.

Above a certain level, scores didn't seem to make much of a difference. In fact, the MIT rep said students trying to achieve perfect test scores were wasting their time. Instead, at this point in the process, she suggested students put that time and effort into getting good grades and writing their essays.

Still, the most selective schools do not expect application essays to be written much differently from those submitted to less selective colleges. In fact, during a college essay panel discussion we moderated, senior admissions staff members from Columbia University and Barnard College said they do not expect better-quality writing from applicants to their schools. They look for reflection and an answer to the prompt. No fancy words. No better writing. Columbia and Barnard—like all schools that require essays for admission—want to know how you think.

Both the Columbia and Barnard reps said the essay was their favorite part of the application package. The task and expectations are the same for just about every college that requires essays.

College Admissions Buzzwords

The college admissions community has its own set of buzzwords. These are words you know, but in the context of applying to college and writing essays, they can be unclear.

What school representatives mean when they speak is often quite different from what you hear. Admissions officers throw out words like passion, voice, leadership, grit, initiative, and authenticity when they speak to prospective students. They may say they look for these traits in their student body.

Let's give this some context.

To you and your friends, passion might sound like something that will drive you to greatness, like building an orphanage or finding a cure for cancer. You might also assume that taking initiative means starting a business or making a cool million before graduation.

Think about the word leadership. What does it mean to you? Does it sound like something that demonstrates your potential to become a world leader, or running for student government president, winning, and then making huge changes in the school?

While these types of experiences could be great for the few who actually have them, this is not what colleges actually mean.

The problem is that the message from the top (admissions) is not making its way down to you, the student. No one is intentionally trying to misguide you. Well-meaning adults, including high school counselors, independent educational consultants, teachers, and parents, try to help. But the message is still not getting conveyed correctly.

It's all part of the reason colleges continue to receive essays that are either boring, don't answer the prompts, or fail to tell them anything new about the student. Those essays, while they may not hurt students, do nothing to enhance the application. Students miss out on an important opportunity to let colleges learn something meaningful about them.

We help our students cut through the chaos. You can do that by breaking down the buzzwords, so you understand what the college essay is, why you have to write one or several, and what admissions officers are looking for. We'll help you start translating the message by exploring one of the most common buzzwords: passion.

Colleges say things like this:

- Show us your passion!

- What is your passion?

- Share your passion.

- Is there something you are so passionate about that your application might be incomplete without it?

Rather than agonize about the word passion, focus on what your audience is asking. Colleges care about core beliefs. To find yours, ask yourself questions like these:

- What do I care about?

- What do I do in my free time?

- What would I do right now if I had nowhere to be and nothing I had to do?

Maybe you walk the dog every day without being asked, or you relax before final exams by drawing cartoon figures. These activities show that you take responsibility or know how to manage stress. Colleges care about that; they care about who you are.

We talked about the mixed messages that permeate admissions offices, and ways to make essays less confusing for students, during a panel discussion at the National Association of College Admission Counseling's annual meeting several years ago. Our panel included top admissions execs from UC-Berkeley and Cornell, as well as two high school counselors—one from a private Jesuit school and one from a large urban public school.

The confusing messages we addressed are still rampant. The counselor from the Jesuit school shared two powerful stories about working with students who found the messages puzzling. We believe his stories will help you understand what colleges mean when they throw out words like leadership and initiative.

The son of a maintenance worker at his school noticed that his high school classmates were leaving the cafeteria in a mess after lunch. The student organized a group of a half-dozen kids who picked up trash so the school's cleaning staff wouldn't be overburdened. He wrote a beautiful essay that demonstrated that he cared about others and knew how to motivate his peers.

Another student came into school one day feeling discouraged because he didn't think he had anything to write about.

The counselor asked his student a few probing questions. He knew the boy played violin and that he volunteered at a senior citizen facility. Asked to describe what he did when he visited, the boy said he played violin there. He and his counselor talked about how he felt when he played for the residents. Because of this conversation, the boy wrote a compelling personal statement about what he learned about himself when he took initiative and played his violin for the seniors during his volunteer shift.

Like our coaches, the counselor knew how to guide the conversation to help draw out his student's best traits so he could find a story to illustrate them. But even with the best of intentions, many adults contribute to the mixed messages that students internalize.

If you can set aside the mixed messages and get some perspective, you will be in a much better position to navigate the application process—and write an effective college application essay that admissions teams will want to read.

Essays won't get a student who is not qualified into any college. But, if you are qualified, they can help you get a better shot at admission to top-choice colleges. Still, even for prepared, hardworking students, applying to college is rarely simple or easy to predict.

One student, Meredith, was accepted to Southern Methodist University business school, plus the University of Miami. She was rejected by Tulane, one of her top choices. She told us that one day, they would be sorry they did not accept her because she was going to own her own company and be super successful.

We spun the story differently for her. We told her she did everything she could, and she wrote wonderful essays that were meaningful and showed who she was.

You only need one school to say yes. Your essays can help you make that case for admission.

CHAPTER 5

A Message for Parents
(+ Dos and Don'ts Guide)

If you are reading this chapter, it's likely your child is preparing to apply to college. You might want to know how you can help your child do that or at least nail the essay.

You've come to the right place.

Wow has been in business a long time. We're intentionally small because we like to give our students the personal attention they need and deserve. That's why we accept a limited number of students to work with us each application season.

We also train high school counselors, independent educational consultants, and other educational professionals on the college essay—the one thing that matters more than you may know and stresses out entire families going through the application process.

We have something for everyone, from this book to free student webinars, informative articles, and private coaching. Our private services are not for every student, but a few of you might be interested. If you're interested and want to see what we have to offer, please visit our website, WowWritingWorkshop.com.

Confused About the College Essay?

Every year, at the beginning of the application season, many parents like you come to us asking for help understanding college application essays. They want to help their children, but they're not sure how. We're parents too. We understand. We know you want to help.

We believe success on the essay can begin at home—sooner rather than later—with you as the guide. As a parent, you know your child better than anyone else. Who else would go to the moon and back to help them prosper as an adult?

What's the first step? Make sure you understand what the college essay is all about.

At its core, the college essay is all about reflection. That is the key to standing out where it matters most—inside the admissions office. The college essay provides students an opportunity to show people who they may never meet just what kind of person they are.

If you have not yet done so, please read Chapter 4, where we clarified the mixed messages that confuse both parents and students and can help you make some sense out of the noise.

Help Your Child Reflect

It's often hard for students to identify their best features. They'd rather talk about accomplishments. At this age, they are not generally known for being reflective. They think about the future: where they will live, what job they might have, or a trip around the world. What's more, most of them have had very little or no practice writing about themselves or being reflective.

You can help your child look inward so they can find meaning in any experience. This is a great opportunity to help your child—and bond a little in the process. The effort can make the difference between a flat essay that bores the admissions office and one that shines. This should make the essay experience much less daunting for the entire family.

Reflection begins with a conversation that you can guide—if you can initiate that conversation without taking it over.

To begin, spend some time thinking about what makes your child so wonderful.

- What do you love about your child?

- What are some of their defining traits and characteristics? Focus on positive qualities, not accomplishments or impressive experiences.

Next, find a time to sit down together, then share and listen with an open mind and heart. This is a journey into self-discovery for your child, where they will identify the characteristics that best define them and think about how they exhibit these traits in the world. If you choose to participate, be patient and kind. If you are not up to this challenge, that's okay too.

If you are game, check your child's schedule and set a time to chat when you know they are not rushed or unduly stressed. Weekends are good. The dinner table can be great. Car rides work, too.

Make sure your child knows what you are doing. This should not be a secret. Keep it casual. Your first task should be easy. Share what you love and admire about your child. What do you brag about to your friends when your child is not around?

After that, ask your child what they consider their best characteristics. If the answer is "I don't know" or "Huh?" try a different question: What do your friends like about you?

Your child might have answers or look at you with confusion. If it seems appropriate, discuss the traits you identified. Listen to—and make sure you hear—the reaction. You may think your child is compassionate, but do they agree with you? If not, why not?

Ask your child to keep thinking about the characteristics that define them, and to consider when and where they exhibit those traits. Your goal is to plant a seed and to help your child understand that colleges know very little about an applicant's character or who they are as a person. Explain that essays offer an opportunity for students to differentiate themselves from other applicants with similar credentials.

At this point, your conversation should be well under way. We don't believe in using a formal script, but we can tell you that this deceptively simple line of questioning gets results. You will be actively engaging in a discussion that could trigger a connection, rather than blank stares.

Guide the conversation. Keep it moving over a series of days or weeks or months. Sit at the kitchen table, in the backyard or go to your favorite coffee shop. Talk for 10 minutes or three hours. It doesn't matter. Just keep talking.

Here are some questions to help you:

- What three words would you use to describe yourself?

- Which three words would your best friend use to describe you to a new student who came to your school?

- What do you like to do when you are not at school?

- What do your friends say about you? Are you a problem-solver? Do you like a challenge?

- I think you are _____ and _____ (list a couple traits). What do you think?

- If you were standing on a stage, and five people you never met were in the audience interviewing you for your dream job, what would you want them to know about you that they couldn't find from reading your resume?

- What makes you great?

You might be pleasantly surprised at the valuable insight and depth you discover by talking about your child's positive characteristics. Getting started is the single biggest challenge. Especially because this task involves getting a teen to sit still for long enough to have a real conversation about something personal and meaningful.

Whatever you do, keep the questions open-ended. Avoid yes-or-no questions. Probe, but do so gently. You can discuss your child's dreams and aspirations later. For now, focus completely on what makes them who they are today—not five years ago or five years from now.

Then, listen to their answers. Those answers will help guide their essay.

A Calm Journey Is the Goal

At Wow, we do our best to keep our students calm as they endure the daunting college application process. Because there is always something going in the world on around us (college admissions scandals, increasing competition at all types of colleges, Covid, concerns about standardized tests), our students and their parents feel a lot of pressure to get into the nation's top colleges.

It's understandable to feel overwhelmed as you try to support your child. But well-intentioned or not, too much help and negative feedback is not constructive and can be emotionally damaging to a 17-year-old who is already stressed out by the college journey. It's nerve-wracking out there. We see it firsthand every application season.

In a college essay, students are asked to do something that even adults can find challenging: reflect on their life experiences. Our students work hard on their essays; we push them as far as we can and encourage them to reflect as much as they can. Sometimes, the final product is a bit rough, but it's genuine and strong. Other times, we find a sweet story that highlights how sensitive and caring a student is. Our favorite essays are perfectly imperfect, just as they should be. They sound like the teens who wrote them.

The disconnect between what colleges want and what others think they want can lead to challenging essay-writing experiences and ineffective essays. Many adults want polish, but colleges want authentic stories showing how students think and what matters to them.

Often, parents, teachers and counselors look specifically for stories that demonstrate leadership, intellect, and initiative, even though that's not what colleges are looking for in a college essay. Colleges want the students to show insight about any trait they believe best represents them. The adults in their lives sometimes think they know what their kids should write about. They don't. We don't. The stories don't sound genuine when adults tell students what to write or how to write it.

We talk about this quite a bit with each other and with counselors like our friend Holly Bennetts, a school counselor and dedicated student advocate in suburban Detroit. We speak together on panels, and she's one of our go-to professionals.

Bennetts works with students on essays every year. She's positive and believes every student's essay needs to sound like the student, be written by the student, and illustrate something meaningful to the student. She is hands-off in her approach, just like us.

But still, Bennetts sees countless students break down in her office every year after their essays are done because a trusted adult in their life (parent, teacher, writer, sibling) suggested their essay was not good enough.

"The student takes that as, 'I am not good enough,'" she says. "It breaks my heart."

It breaks our hearts, too.

We hear stories like this all the time. Too many parents offer feedback and mark up essays in a way that only makes students feel sad.

It's not acceptable for any adult to second-guess a student's essay topic, polish the essay or, even worse, write a college essay for them.

Please don't do that.

If you do, your child will walk away with a negative message: *I am not good enough.*

We know you don't want that for your child. We don't, either.

Trust us, if you can help your child reflect and identify positive characteristics, you've done more than enough to prepare them to answer a college application prompt.

What Happened When a Mom
Overstepped Her Role?

The night before an early application deadline, a client named Jessica called us in a panic.

What if my son doesn't get into his top-choice college because his essay lacks sophistication, or sounds like an immature 17-year-old?

Her son's essay was excellent. It was proofed and ready to submit. He described himself as someone who had a hard time relaxing, and his essay was about the night he learned to "just let it go" while doing a stand-up routine at a comedy club. The story was frank and honest, and it hit the mark. He showed how he learned to calm himself. It was funny, too. Best of all, it sounded like the smart 17-year-old who wrote it.

Was it sophisticated? No. Was it mature? Relatively speaking, sure. But not like an adult. Did it sound professional? No way. It's not supposed to sound professional or like an adult.

The boy answered the prompt, demonstrated insight, and wrote it himself. His high school counselor liked it, too.

However, as the deadline got closer, Jessica began to panic. She passed the essay around to other adults, including a few writers and editors she trusted, even though none of them had any experience with the college admissions process or essay coaching. What's worse, her friends were critical, saying the essay was immature and pedestrian. They were wrong, but Jessica started to believe them.

She marked up the essay with a pen, suggested word changes, and rewrote complete sentences to help the writing flow. She showed us the finished product and insisted that the piece still maintained the essence of his voice. We disagreed.

Essence of a voice doesn't count. Jessica took her son's voice away.

We calmly explained why her son should submit the version we proofread before she marked it all up and ruined it. We didn't mince words. She admitted he was upset when she showed him her edited draft. We told her that she shattered his confidence.

Jessica acknowledged her error in judgment. To her credit, she ultimately encouraged him to submit his original essay (and he was eventually accepted to his top-choice school).

Jessica did not intend to make her son feel bad; she apologized to him. But he could not unhear her harsh words, nor could he unsee the negative comments on his college essay. The damage had already been done.

To avoid situations like this one, you should always have a process and trust it. We've shared some of our process throughout the book to help guide you.

Ready to Guide Your Child?

A few years ago, we got a call from Deb, a normally calm and even-keeled mom. She said she was fit to be tied. She wanted out of the college essay coaching job she'd given herself while her daughter was applying to college.

Deb thought she could handle the job alone. But that didn't work out so well.

Soon after they began working together on the first essay, a personal statement, Deb's daughter began pushing back, creating noticeable tension inside their home. Car rides and family meals were unpleasant. Deb called Wow when she was at her wit's end.

"I always felt confident that I could help my kids with their schoolwork, but when it came to the college essays, there was just too much emotion involved," Deb said. "I knew my daughter needed guidance, but I could not be the one to give it to her."

You don't want to behave like the mom who marked up her son's essay. But you don't have to feel like Deb did during your child's journey to college, either.

You can avoid some of the stress if you help your child start the process early.

As part of a low-stress environment that allows them to succeed, your child needs a process, plan, and schedule.

We give all our students a schedule, along with a step-by-step process to get the essay done effectively without losing momentum. We provide students with simple tasks and break them down into bite-sized assignments that make the writing process manageable.

It was not Deb's fault that she didn't have a process. She didn't know she was making things worse for her daughter.

We were able to give Deb and her daughter the tools their family needed to succeed.

Was her daughter stressed anymore? Nope.

Did she feel confident? Absolutely.

Did she feel proud of her essay when it was done? Yes.

And did she get into her first-choice school? She did.

The college essay was so daunting for Deb, for the other boy's mom, and for so many parents just like you. Why? Because it matters a lot.

We want to help you give your child an environment that is designed for success. One that is calm. Nurturing. Quiet.

We're a virtual company with private coaching services. We help our families keep the essay under control—no matter what's going on in the world around us.

We developed our own process, called the Wow Method, which is the most effective process out there because we've spent more than 10 years perfecting it. We challenge ourselves every day. We hire the best coaches. We ask questions and dig deep.

We know the word "process" isn't particularly enticing or flashy. But that shouldn't matter. Our process works with every type of student in every type of situation. (We explain the process in Chapter 3.)

Wow's approach is simple, with clear instructions, which is exactly what you need to help your child succeed. Our writing coaches use our virtual communication tools to streamline the process and make it easy for students to write effective college essays.

Wow is now well into our second decade in business, and we are grateful to our students and professional clients. During the off-season, we train independent educational consultants, counselors, and other professionals who are on the ground, working with students every day. We are essay coaches to the essay coaches.

What's our secret? We are teachers and writers who understand our customers' needs and their audience. We talk to admissions officers all the time. We know what they want, and we know how to deliver it. We are process focused. Your child can get some of our expertise in our book. But it won't take the place of one-on-one coaching.

We can teach any child how to write strong, effective essays, with less stress and greater confidence for them. If that's what you want, please let us know.

Meanwhile, we encourage you to read the entire book with a mindful eye. As you read, consider that there are some

4,300 two- and four-year colleges in the U.S. They recruit. They offer scholarships. Keep your eyes and ears open, and you might find a prize in a school you did not know existed.

We know that as a parent, you worry about your child. We worry about our own children too. That's a big part of the job. But when your child is applying to college, it's not healthy to get too wrapped up in the process. This is your child's journey.

If you are worried, just acknowledge you are concerned and try hard to bite your tongue.

Help your child feel good about this writing process and encourage them to own it. Above all, parents need to help their children trust themselves, feel confident, and proudly share their stories.

Just in case you need a reminder on how to be as supportive as possible, without overstepping, we're including a list of some of the biggest dos and don'ts below.

College Essay Dos and Don'ts for Parents

DO:

- Do behave like a cheerleader, not a coach.

- Do talk to your child about positive traits and characteristics you like about them.

- Do ask your child what's important to them.

- Do share encouraging words with your child.

- Do stay positive.

DON'T:

- Don't tell your child which prompt to select.

- Don't tell your child which trait you think colleges prefer in prospective students.

- Don't tell your child what to write, which topic you think will work best, or which words to use.

- Don't say the essay does not matter or that admissions representatives don't read them.

- Don't be discouraging or negative.

- Don't write or "fix" the essay yourself.

CHAPTER 6

Resources

This chapter features resources to help you start the college essay writing process.

1. Dos and Don'ts

2. What Do the Common App Prompts Really Mean?

3. Tips from Inside the Admissions Office

4. 5 Myths and Facts of College Essays

5. Testimonials from Wow Students

1. College Essay Dos and Don'ts for Students

Do:

- Do follow the instructions and answer the prompt.

- Do check the prompt's word/character limit.

- Do write about yourself; you are impressive.

- Do explore why your story matters to you.

- Do show insight into your character and demonstrate reflection.

- Do share something meaningful colleges do not already know about you.

- Do illustrate a positive trait.

- Do write the essay yourself.

- Do write it in your own voice, using the words you use every day.

- Do check spelling and grammar before you click send.

Don't:

- Don't write about someone other than yourself.

- Don't focus on your accomplishments or experiences.

- Don't write something that illustrates a negative trait.

- Don't write what you think colleges want to read.

- Don't plagiarize or let anyone write the essay (or a piece of it) for you.

- Don't imitate sample essays you find in books or on the internet.

- Don't believe everything you read: There are no gimmicks, tricks, or shortcuts to help you master the essay.

- Don't repeat the question in your answer or overuse buzzwords (passion, grit, leadership, etc.).

- Don't rely on spellcheck or a grammar checker.

2. What Do the Common App Prompts Really Mean?

Every few years, the Common Application, a tool used by hundreds of colleges to help students apply seamlessly to multiple schools, makes noticeable changes to its essay prompts. The changes are based on feedback from students, parents, high school counselors, educational consultants, and colleges following each admissions cycle.

In 2021, the Common App retired a seldom-used prompt about solving a problem and replaced it with a prompt to allow students to write about the positive influence of other people in their lives. The prompt reads:

Reflect on something that someone has done for you that has made you happy or thankful in a surprising way. How has this gratitude affected or motivated you?

The Common App said this new prompt was inspired by scientific research on gratitude and kindness during a global pandemic. They hoped the prompt might validate the importance of kindness and gratitude; they look at this prompt as an invitation to bring some joy into their application experience.

It's imperative that you know that admissions officers do not favor this prompt (or any prompt) over another. Pick one you like that speaks to you, and one you can answer with relative ease. We've parsed, or broken down and analyzed, this prompt below, as well as the other six.

You may recall how to read and understand a prompt from Chapter 2. As a refresher, review these instructions for the personal statement on the Common Application:

The essay demonstrates your ability to write clearly and concisely on a selected topic and helps you distinguish yourself in your own voice. What do you want the readers of your application to know about you apart from courses, grades, and test scores? Choose the option that best helps you answer that question and write an essay of no more than 650 words, using the prompt to inspire and structure your response. Remember: 650 words is your limit, not your goal. Use the full range if you need it, but don't feel obligated to do so. (The application won't accept a response shorter than 250 words.)

No matter which essay prompt you choose, before you start brainstorming ideas, think about what you want readers to know about you. The question is not "What do they want to hear?" or "What should I write?" Instead, answer this: "What do I want readers to know about me that they couldn't find out from the rest of my application?" They know that you are on the debate team or that you play soccer. They know that you got a B+ in algebra or scored well on the ACT (if you submit your score). What they don't know is whether you are creative, decisive, determined, self-motivated, or cautious. They don't know how your experiences have shaped you. Your essay offers an opportunity to consider what you want them to know and remember.

Here's our take on the seven options, including Prompt 4, the gratitude prompt, straight from Wow, the virtual platform we use with our students. We make sure our private coaching students understand the prompts before they dive in and draft an essay. It saves them a lot of time on unnecessary drafts that might miss the mark.

Prompt 1
Some students have a background, identity, interest, or talent that is so meaningful they believe their application would be incomplete without it. If this sounds like you, then please share your story.

The key word in this prompt is "meaningful."

To answer this prompt effectively, consider why your background, identity, interest, or talent is significant to you. Colleges are more concerned with who you are than your background, identity, interest, or talent. What does your talent illustrate about you? What have you learned about yourself because of your background?

At its core, the college essay is all about reflection. What do you want readers to know about you after reading your essay? Why does it matter to you? In your response, you will need to focus on why something is meaningful to you, and make sure it answers the prompt.

You could respond to this prompt by sharing insight gained from any background, identity, interest, or talent—a significant conversation, or a moment when you realized something important about yourself—anything that truly and vividly demonstrates who you are and answers the prompt in a thoughtful manner. Your experience does not have to be particularly impressive. You do not have to write about what you learned while climbing a mountain or how you got over your fear of fires after rescuing three children from a burning building. You could write about how you developed compassion for older people while making meatballs with your grandma or how you became more confident after navigating a car on an icy highway. Your challenge is to find an idea that illustrates something meaningful. Choose a single moment or focus on an idea, and then explore it in detail.

Prompt 2

The lessons we take from obstacles we encounter can be fundamental to later success. Recount a time when you faced a challenge, setback, or failure. How did it affect you, and what did you learn from the experience?

Prompt 2 is more specific than 1. In this case, the key sentence is at the end of this prompt: "How did it affect you, and what did you learn from the experience?" Your readers are not going to judge you because you had a setback or failed at something. Everyone faces obstacles. The intent of the prompt is to help you reflect on how you deal with unexpected complications and disappointments; that insight can be incredibly revealing.

Answering this prompt requires you to think more broadly about challenges and setbacks, reflect on the experience, and demonstrate how you grew or changed as a result. It's best to focus on the solution, not the problem. Keep the story positive.

What do you want readers to know about you? Have you faced a challenge, setback, or failure that shows you are resilient or demonstrates that you learned to be a leader? Are you the kind of person who can turn every difficult experience into something positive? If this sounds like you, this may be a good prompt to choose.

Prompt 3
Reflect on a time when you questioned or challenged a belief or idea. What prompted your thinking? What was the outcome?

Prompt 3 also asks for reflection. It is one of the most specific prompts and requires you to share how you think in a deeper way than some of the other prompts. In this case, the central story should showcase a time when you challenged a belief or idea. Maybe you raised your hand in class at your religious school and said you did not believe in God. Why did you do that? What happened? What did you learn about yourself? Perhaps you challenged a family rule or a school dress code. Did you challenge something you had always believed in or question something you had long felt uncomfortable with?

When has your opinion been unpopular? Why do you stand up for what you believe in? What is so important to you that you feel the need to challenge authority? Why? What inspires you to take action?

During high school, you are constantly asked to look toward the future: Where are you going? What do you want to do with your life? Where will you attend college? What career will you pursue? Your college application essay offers an opportunity to look back, and this prompt is a prime example.

If you are a deep thinker who asks a lot of questions, loves to play the devil's advocate, challenges authority, or questions religious and other dogma, this might be a good prompt for you.

Prompt 4

Reflect on something that someone has done for you that has made you happy or thankful in a surprising way. How has this gratitude affected or motivated you?

On the surface, Prompt 4 seems to be asking about a time you felt gratitude. But it's not quite so simple. This prompt is both reflective and very specific. The key words here are reflect, surprising, gratitude, affected, and motivated.

This prompt invites you to reflect on someone else's action, but the story you tell should not be primarily about the other person's act. It should be about how this experience affected you. What changed for you, or what did you do differently as a result?

And the prompt doesn't ask you to share just any act of kindness. Readers want to know about something someone did for you that made you happy or thankful in a surprising way. Maybe the other person surprised you with their kindness, or maybe you were surprised that you felt so grateful or happy. Or maybe the surprise came through in some other way.

If you can identify a specific story that focuses on you, showcases a characteristic or trait that demonstrates who you are, fits these criteria, and also explains how your gratitude affected or motivated you to do something, this prompt might be for you.

Prompt 5

Discuss an accomplishment, event, or realization that sparked a period of personal growth and a new understanding of yourself or others.

Prompt 5 is more specific, but still leaves room for reflection and interpretation. This prompt asks you to discuss something you accomplished, an experience you've had, or something that sparked growth and understanding. Remember, you do not have to show that you mastered something challenging to answer this prompt effectively. Rather, you are being asked to demonstrate how you have grown from your accomplishment, personal growth, or insight. What do you know or understand now that you didn't know before?

Colleges want to know about you, not the experience. What did you learn from your accomplishment, event, or realization? Why was it significant? What do you want readers to know about you? Think traits and characteristics, not accomplishments, not events, and not realizations.

The best answer will illustrate the traits and characteristics you want to share with colleges, show insight into your character, and answer the prompt.

Prompt 6

Describe a topic, idea, or concept you find so engaging that it makes you lose all track of time. Why does it captivate you? What or who do you turn to when you want to learn more?

The key word in Prompt 6 is "engaging." This prompt asks about your intellectual curiosity. What motivates you? How and where do you get information? What do you do with it? Why?

The college essay is as much a thinking task as it is a writing task; readers want to know how you think in this and any prompt. What gets you excited? What energizes you? What makes you tick?

Think about who you are. Maybe you care about social justice. Perhaps you're captivated by humor or technology. Is it football? Do you get lost in a good book? A family dinner discussion about world events? Do you scream at the TV during a political debate? How do you learn? The internet? Your favorite teacher?

Try asking yourself questions like these: Why is this topic, idea, or concept so engaging? How does it make me feel? Who do I talk to about these ideas? Where do I go to research new concepts?

How resourceful are you when your curiosity is piqued to the fullest? The answer to this prompt should also reveal something to admissions about the breadth or depth of your interests.

You can explore the big-picture concept overall or share an example of that concept in action. Whether you collected clothes and toiletries for a local family who lost their home in a fire or attracted 10,000 followers by tweeting a daily joke, the real story will come to life if you can explain why you did it.

Prompt 7

Share an essay on any topic of your choice. It can be one you've already written, one that responds to a different prompt, or one of your own design.

The key word in this prompt is "choice." And while this prompt appears to be different from the others, the purpose is the same. Yes, applicants can submit any essay they want, but as the overall instructions clearly state, even an A+ paper must still illustrate something meaningful about you and show reflection.

Suppose you want to submit a critical analysis you wrote for Honors English about a character in *Jane Eyre*. Could it work? Maybe. Ask yourself what the essay demonstrates about you. Do you yearn for more than what traditional society allows, like Jane? Does the paper demonstrate how the book propelled you toward political activism? Does it show how the book changed you? After admissions officers read the paper, will they learn something new about you? If not, it won't work as a college essay, no matter how well-written.

Write about yourself—about what you love, where you come from, what you aspire to, how you spend your time, what bugs you, what inspires you. In any case, consider what you want admissions to know about you that can help fill in the unknown details needed to enhance your application package. What do they know? What do you want them to know?

We've said this several times, and we're going to say it again: Colleges are interested in the traits that make you who you are, not the experiences or activities that are highlighted elsewhere on your application.

As with all prompts for any type of personal statement, the college essay is all about reflection. If you choose this prompt, make sure you tell a focused story about you that shows insight into your character and provides information that colleges wouldn't know about you from the rest of the application.

3. Tips from Inside the Admissions Office

Time and again, admissions officers tell us exactly what they want in the essays. Their advice is worth listening to.

Students often think the personal statement must be a discussion of their most traumatic experiences. Admissions officers from every type of school tell us over and again that it's okay if you have lived a relatively peaceful existence. They want to learn about who you are. As long as you answer the prompt and share something meaningful about yourself, you can write about almost anything.

John Ambrose, Director of Undergraduate Admissions at Michigan State University

"I look for genuineness of character, unique flair of personality, identifiable traits of a leader or follower, team player and someone who has the capacity to add to the rich diversity of our campus and our traditions. Be your most authentic self. Students put a lot of effort into trying to convince admissions officers who they think we want to see. But authenticity is always appreciated."

Kim Bryant, Assistant Director of Admissions at the University of Michigan

"This is your interview. Let me know who you really are."

Heath Einstein, Dean of Admission at Texas Christian University

"Don't get hung up on the right topic. Most 17-year-olds haven't scaled Kilimanjaro, so don't worry about finding an angle that hasn't been tried before. Write about what you know. If the most meaningful experience to you has been serving as a camp counselor, it doesn't matter that other students have addressed it. People will try to talk you out of certain ideas but trust your gut. Ultimately, be yourself, and that will be good enough."

Lorenzo Gamboa, Director of Diversity, Inclusion, and Outreach at Santa Clara University

"Students do not need to compile an entire season into an essay. Just give us one place, one time, one moment, and that will do it for you. The key is to show genuine passion, commitment and that they have what it takes to survive at the school."

Christoph Guttentag, Dean of Undergraduate Admissions at Duke University

"By the time [the application] comes to us, many of them have gone through so many hands that the essays are sanitized. I wish I saw more of a thoughtful voice of a 17-year-old."

Christina Lopez, Dean of Enrollment Management at Barnard College

"The whole application process is one big 'Match.com' process. The students are creating their profile within their application and reflecting in the essays on who they are as scholars and people."

Stefanie Niles, President at Cottey College

"An essay doesn't have to be long to be a high-quality piece, but care needs to be taken to answer the question you are asked, and to be thoughtful in both what you say and how you say it. I've seen lots of careless mistakes, like misspelling the name of the major you wish to pursue. I've also seen too many students write an essay as if they were writing a text, without capitalizing words and using little punctuation. But the biggest mistake is not putting in the appropriate effort to write the very best essay you can."

Tamara Siler, Rice University, Deputy Director of Admission, Access and Inclusion at Rice University

"Focus on a moment you feel has defined you as a person, and as a student. As more students who might identify as first generation to attend college, low-income, ethnically diverse, and/or LGBTQ+, the essay allows them to bring even more of their voice and perspectives to the selection table."

Gregory Sneed, Vice President for Enrollment Management at Denison University

"Even after reviewing a mediocre transcript or seeing a limited activities list, I can be swayed to admit a student who writes an essay who really blows me away. The topic of the essay doesn't need to be mind-blowing (in fact, the most mundane topics are often the most relatable and enjoyable), but if it reveals someone who would be highly valued in our campus community, that could tip the scales."

Calvin Wise, Director of Recruitment at Johns Hopkins University

"The essay does not have to be about something huge, some life-changing event. You can write about an aha moment, what defines you as a person. But it doesn't have to be extensive.

Students think they need a monumental experience, but the essay can be about something small. What does it mean to you? That is what we want to know."

4. 5 Myths and Facts of College Essays

Before you start writing, consider these myths and facts surrounding the college essay:

Myth #1: *No one really reads the application essays.*
Fact: *Of course, admission officers read your college essays.*
Colleges wouldn't ask you to write something they did not plan to read.

Over the years, we have asked dozens of admissions representatives if they really read college essays. A few years ago, we even polled admissions reps during a national conference on this subject. The collective answer is always yes.

Myth #2: *An application essay must be written about an impressive topic.*
Fact: *You are impressive, not the topic.*
The subject is you; the topic is important but secondary. A college application essay is your opportunity to share something meaningful about yourself. Colleges care more about who you are than what you did.

Many of our students come to us with topics in mind. One young woman started the process confident that discussing a trip to help the poor in Central America would impress admissions officers. It was a big trip, and she was sure someone would want to read about it. Using our writing process, the student realized that her most important personal moment occurred during that service trip, when she overcame her fear of heights by jumping off a cliff into water. She wrote a gorgeous, meaningful story that showed what she learned about herself during the terrifying jump.

Her essay was not about some huge, life-changing event. Rather, she anchored her story around a specific moment when she faced her fear and learned that she was brave. It was a small story that illustrated something significant to her.

Myth #3: *Your personal statement for college should sound sophisticated, like Hemingway or a professor.*
Fact: *Admission officers do not expect you to sound like a professional writer.*
The college essay is your story and only yours. You are a high school junior or senior, and you should sound like one. Not your mom. Not your dad. Not your English teacher. And certainly not one of the most revered writers of all time!

We can tell when we read an essay that does not match the student's voice. We can tell if students use a thesaurus or experiment with language. We also know when adults overstep. And, if you think admissions committees don't know if you get too much help, or if an adult polishes your work, you are in for a surprise. They know. They don't like it, either. What's more, if someone writes an essay for you or you plagiarize, admissions officers can tell, and they might automatically reject your application if they even suspect it.

Myth #4: *There is a right way and a wrong way to write an essay.*
Fact: *Your best story will grow out of the process of writing your college application essay.*
There are no gimmicks, magic formulas, tricks, or shortcuts to writing the perfect college application essay. Perfect is not the goal. Just trust the process. We break our process down into small, manageable steps that will free you up to focus on what

matters most: finding and writing stories in your own words and in your own voice.

Colleges just want to get to know you, so give them something honest and real so they can dig deeper and find out more about who you are. In most cases, the essay is your only opportunity to speak directly to admissions decision-makers during the application process.

Myth #5: *Only superstar students impress admissions officers with their essays.*

Fact: *Anyone can stand out with a meaningful story that answers the prompt.*

You certainly don't have to rescue a child from a house fire, find a cure for cancer, get a million downloads for an app you developed, or train seeing-eye dogs to impress admissions officers. Some of the best essays we've read over the years have been anchored around mundane moments: a girl who found her passion for nature while pulling weeds in a community garden, and a boy who discovered his problem-solving skills when he forgot his cello for an orchestra concert and improvised his performance with a bass guitar.

5. Praise from Wow Students and How to Reserve a Wow Coach

It can be hard to write about yourself, especially when the stakes seem so high. Our simple process, The Wow Method, helps students write strong, effective essays with confidence.

If you think you might want to work with our coaches, please visit our website, *WowWritingWorkshop.com/Undergrad*, to learn about our different coaching plans and see what we have to offer. We make the writing process as manageable as possible, helping students write genuine, effective essays that admissions officers want to read.

You will also find additional resources, including college essay blogs and our free monthly webinar for students. It's easy to sign up, and it's okay if you can't join us live. We'll send you a recording of the webinar.

See what our former students have to say about Wow:

Josh S.
"Here is what I liked about the writing process: I liked that we didn't get into the actual essay itself right away. The writing exercises that I did prior to starting the first draft made writing the actual essay much easier."

Emma N.
"I liked working with Wow because I felt like I was in charge of my essay. The final product of my essay sounded just like me. It's a really personal story and you can tell a lot about who I am from the story and my voice."

Miriam L.

"When I was accepted to the University of Michigan the head of admissions called me and told me that my essays were so good that she was going to keep them. She said she could really hear my voice in my writing and that I should pursue writing in college."

Josie S.

"I loved working with you and Wow! I loved the organization of the steps to writing my perfect essay. You really helped me develop my ideas and mold it into a perfect essay to show admissions another side of myself."

William S.

"I really enjoyed working with you and am very pleased with how my essay turned out. I liked the whole process. I thought my schedule was very well distributed, and I never felt stressed at any time."

Marni J.

"Thank you so much for all of the time, hard work, and dedication you put into helping me write my essays. You showed me how to find my own writing voice. I learned so much from you through this process; you have truly inspired me to trust myself and continue writing with confidence."

Sarah G.

"This has been such a valuable resource for me. The best part about the Wow program was how manageable and effective each of the steps were. I enjoyed how varied the steps and exercises were because each one helped me discover more about how I wanted to construct my essay. The skills will definitely be useful for me in the future too!"

Grant D.
"I liked how each step in the Wow Method built on the last so that the essay continued to grow and improve. Instructions were clear and provided specific details on how to problem solve and revise, which was helpful."

Regan D.
"You made my college application process so much easier, and I am forever grateful!"

Quinn H.
"When it came to the Wow process, I liked how well the writing exercises all translated and found their way into writing my actual essay. It was a good feeling knowing that whatever exercise I did it would end up directly improving my essay."

Elana W.
"Thank you for everything, for your support, advice, useful tips, and for believing in me. You have been unbelievably helpful. You are the best!"

ABOUT WOW

Authors Kim Lifton and Susan Knoppow are the co-founders of Wow Writing Workshop, which teaches students and educational professionals a simple, step-by-step process for writing effective college essays so students can stand out and tell their stories. They are members or affiliates of the Michigan Association of College Admission Counseling (MACAC), the National Association of College Admission Counseling (NACAC), the Independent Educational Consultants Association (IECA), and the Higher Education Consultants Association (HECA). They write and speak regularly to high school, parent, and professional groups about the role of the college essay within the competitive admissions world. Before launching Wow, Susan and Kim collaborated on multiple projects, including the award-winning PBS documentary, *No Ordinary Joe: Erasing the Stigma of Mental Illness*. Their books on the college essay have become go-to resources for families and counselors around the world.

Kim Lifton, President

Perceptive, resourceful, and curious, Kim can get a story out of anyone; she helped create the brainstorming process used in the Wow Method. Kim's articles on the college essay appear regularly in print and on the web, and her work has been featured in a variety of newspapers, magazines, and online publica-

tions. Kim is a former newspaper reporter and corporate communications manager with a BA in Journalism from Michigan State University.

Susan Knoppow, CEO

Focused, incisive, and creative, Susan can turn the most daunting writing challenge into a series of simple steps; she conceptualized and developed the Wow Method for teaching writing.

A former executive speechwriter and copywriter, Susan is also a published poet and essayist. She holds a BA

in Psychology from the University of Michigan and an MFA in Writing from Vermont College.